Explore Green Men is the first detailed study of the history of this motif for 25 years. Dr MacDermott's research follows the Green Man back from the previous earliest known examples into its hitherto unrecognised origins in India more than two thousand years ago.

The book starts by discussing the 'paganization' of Green Men in recent decades, then traces them back through the Victorian Gothic Revival and the Italianate periods, to their heyday in the Gothic and their supposed origins in the Romanesque. For every period there is background information on the cultural changes that affected how Green Men were regarded. The author also discusses the comparisons that have been made with Cernunnus, Robin Hood, Jack-in-the-Green, woodwoses, Baphomet, Al Khidr and Bulgarian *peperuda*. She also investigates which pagan god Green Men supposedly represent.

Explore Green Men is illustrated with 118 photographs and drawings, mostly of Green Men who have never before showed their faces in books. This second edition contains a summary of independent confirmation of the links with Asia.

This book will appeal to all with an interest in Green Men and to art historians looking for a reliable study of this fascinating decorative motif.

Mercia MacDermott read Russian at Oxford and then specialized in Bulgarian history and culture. Her previous publications include studies of Bulgarian folk customs and national liberation movements against Ottoman rule. She researched Green Men for over seven years before writing this book.

Ruth Wylie trained in art and photography. During the 1980s, alerted to Kathleen Basford's book *The Green Man*, she began cataloguing sightings reported by other researchers and has travelled extensively in Britain and Europe to photograph many of these carvings.

The aim of Heart of Albion's 'Explore' series is to provide accessible introductions to folklore and mythology. Some books will provide overviews of quite broad topics, drawing together current academic research with popular beliefs. Other books in the series will deal with more specific topics, but still with the aim of providing a wide-ranging introduction to the topic.

Series editor: Bob Trubshaw

Other titles in the 'Explore' series include:

Explore Folklore Bob Trubshaw

Explore Mythology Bob Trubshaw

Explore Shamanism Alby Stone

Explore Fairy Traditions Jeremy Harte

Explore Phantom Black Dogs edited by Bob Trubshaw

Explore Dragons Richard Freeman

Explore Hinduism Bansi Pandit

EXPLORE GREEN MEN

second edition

Mercia MacDermott

Photographs by Ruth Wylie

Heart of Albion

Explore Green Men

2nd edition

Mercia MacDermott

Photographs by Ruth Wylie

Front cover: A spandrel from a chapel in the
south choir aisle of the cathedral of St Andrew,
Bordeaux; fourteenth or fifteenth century.
Photograph by Ruth Wylie.

ISBN 1 872883 94 X
EAN 978-1-872883-946

Explore Books
An imprint of Heart of Albion Press
2 Cross Hill Close, Wymeswold
Loughborough, LE12 6UJ

albion@indigogroup.co.uk

Visit our Web site: www.hoap.co.uk

Printed in the UK by Booksprint

To the memory of our good friend
Kathleen Basford, who brought us
together and inspired us to
question and explore.

CONTENTS

1 IN SEARCH OF GREEN MEN   1
     Finding Green Men. Interpreting Green Men   1
     Interpreting Green Men   1
     Some contrasting approaches to the Green Man   3

2 SOME SUPPOSED ALIASES OF THE GREEN MAN   9
     Cernunnus, King Arthur and Robin Hood   10
     The tale of Sir Gawain and the Green Knight   11
     Al-Khidr – the 'Green One'   14
     Jack-in-the-Green   15
     The *Peperuda* in Bulgaria   17
     The May King and May festivities   19

3 THE GOTHIC REVIVAL   23
     Two key questions for explorers   23
     The Victorian Background   25
     Victorian Green Men   27

4 FROM THE RENAISSANCE TO ROMANTICISM   31
     The Renaissance   31
     The Reformation   34
     The Counter-Reformation   34
     The Enlightenment   37
     Romanticism   37
     Gardens during the Renaissance and after   38
     Green Men 'reborn'   42
     Green Men on tombs and memorials   47
     Secular and domestic Green Men   52
     Gren Men abroad   61
     The Wildman or Woodwose   63
     Some conclusions   68

5 THE GOTHIC AGE AND ITS GREEN MEN   71
     The essence and origin of Gothic style   71
     Mediaeval society   73
     Mediaeval gardens and attitudes towards Nature   80
     The leaves of Southwell   82
     Where to look and what to look for   89
     What we can learn from mediaeval best-sellers   101

6 THE ROMANESQUE AGE AND ITS FOLIATE HEADS   113
    Some historical background   113
    The rise of monasteries   118
    The importance of pilgrimages   122
    Romanesque sculpture as a whole   125
    Where to look and what you will find   138

7 PRE-ROMANESQUE DISCOVERIES AND DEAD ENDS 155
    The foliate heads of the Dark Ages   155
    Pagan deities and pagan survivals   157
    The Green Man and the Knights Templar   165
    A passing glance at the Anglo-Saxons   166
    Where do disgorging heads come from?   166

8 THE INDIAN CONNECTION   169
    The kirttimukha and the makara   169
    Parallels between Indian and Romanesque art   176
    How Indian motifs reached the West   182
    Triple hares   185
    The Buddhist connection   186
    Triple Hares and Green Men   187
    The Viking connection   187

9 UNDERSTANDING GREEN MEN   192
    Foliate heads and folklore   192
    A look at symbolism and their uses   193
    Journey's end and future goals   198

BIBLIOGRAPHY   200

INDEX   203

*Four Green Men and the Scottish lion on a roof-boss in the
Chapter House of Glenluce Abbey, Dumfries and Galloway.
Sixteenth century. Photo: Ruth Wylie.*

ACKNOWLEDGEMENTS

We are deeply grateful to all the deans, chapters, vicars, curators and other custodians of Green Men whose kindness and co-operation made it possible to produce this book. We would also like to thank the Bildarchiv Foto Marburg; British Library; Churches Conservation Trust; Dorset Natural History and Archaeological Society at the Dorset County Museum; the Museo Arqueológico Nacional, Madrid; The Museum of Fine Arts, Boston; Principal of St Edmund Hall, Oxford; *Science* and the American Association for the Advancement of Science; the State Administration of Cultural Heritage, People's Republic of China; Sussex Archaeological Museum; Thames and Hudson; Victoria and Albert Picture Library; Benoy B. Behl; Ivo Hadzhimishev; Spaska Paskova (Director of the Historical Museum in Gotsé Delchev, Bulgaria), who went personally to the Rozhen Monastery to photograph the Green Man for this book; Tina Negus; Anne Tarver, David Taylor; Helen Ward; Stephen Weeks; and all the other individuals who made their photographs available to us and who helped in various ways.

A capital in the nave of the church of St Andoche, Saulieu, Côte d'Or, Burgundy. Twelfth century. Photo: Ruth Wylie.

1: IN SEARCH OF GREEN MEN

Finding Green Men

Strange leafy faces may stare back at us if we look carefully at the details of most cathedrals and many ancient parish churches. Sometimes the face is composed entirely of leaves; sometimes sprays of foliage issue from the mouth, nose, forehead, or even eyes. Its expression may range from sad, anguished, tormented or downright sinister to benign and almost jovial. Sometimes it peers out through petals or greenery, scowling, or serene, or smiling like a Cheshire Cat; sometimes it actually has a cat's face, and sometimes there is no real face at all, but just an arrangement of leaves whose indentations suggest a mouth, nose and eyes.

All these leafy faces are commonly supposed to be aspects of the Green Man – an image so potent and mysterious that some people, having once set eyes upon it, become as addicted to the pursuit of fresh sightings as spotters of birds and trains.

Discovering Green Men is comparatively easy, since, unlike birds and trains, they conveniently stay put for centuries on end. They are, moreover, not confined to ecclesiastical buildings, but can also be found in a great variety of secular and domestic settings, from streets and gardens to suits of armour, tapestries and table-legs. They know no frontiers, and lurk in countries as far apart as China and Spain, as well as in most of those in between. We merely have to keep our eyes open, and searching for Green Men can add purpose and excitement to sightseeing.

Interpreting Green Men

Many enthusiasts are content simply to be 'Green Man spotters', checking off lists and recording new examples. Others want to delve deeper and discover the hidden meaning behind the enigmatical leafy faces. This is a far more difficult and tricky undertaking. There are virtually no clues in contemporary historical documents to guide us in our quest. We cannot even be sure of the name given to the images by those who commissioned them or carried out the work.

The now familiar term 'Green Man' is, in the context of church carving, a comparatively recent invention, dating only from 1939 when it was introduced by Lady Raglan in an article published in *Folklore*. Here she expresses the opinion that the motif represents an archetypal 'green' folk-figure, whom she identifies with Jack-in-the-

Chancel arch respond in the church of St Mary the Virgin, Finedon, Northamptonshire. Fourteenth century. Photo: Ruth Wylie.

Green, Robin Hood, the May King and the Garland. The term 'Green Man' caught on, probably because it was both straightforward and evocative, and because growing interest in the image required that it had a name. Thus, nowadays, the name is accepted and used by everyone, including those who are sceptical about Lady Raglan's conclusions.

Explorers should, however, be wary of basing any theories on a name that is not only new, but also purely English. The terms used in other countries where the motif occurs are likely to be totally different. Present-day French writers, for example, usually describe Green Men as *masques de feuilles* (leaf-masks) or *masques feuillus* (foliate masks). By so doing they are following the tradition of a rare written reference to the motif. This occurs in an illustrated architectural notebook compiled by the thirteenth-century master mason, Villard de Honnecourt. He shows four examples of foliate heads: two in which the leaves seem to be sprouting like hair and beards from otherwise human heads, and two in which leaves, with stalks instead of necks, have acquired eyes, noses, mouths and other human features. De Honnecourt refers to both types as *têtes de feuilles* (leaf heads). We do not know whether he used the same term to describe heads disgorging sprigs and sprays, because these are not illustrated in his notebook, although they certainly existed at the time.

Explorers eager to get to the root of things may find 'foliate heads' a better and more accurate term than 'Green Man', but we appear to be stuck with the popular name, even though it can give rise to misconceptions and confusion.

In one form or another, foliate heads have been around for centuries, even millennia. In recent years, however, the motif has, as it were, been 're-discovered', and now attracts a great deal of attention. Groups and individuals, justifiably alarmed by certain negative aspects of modern 'progress' and 'development', and by the growing threat to the natural environment, have adopted the Green Man as their emblem. In the process they have invested the image with significance and meanings of their own choosing. These may or may not reflect the intentions of the original carvers. For example, what some people today like to regard as a symbol of our unity with Nature may at times have been perceived by our mediaeval ancestors as a warning against becoming entangled in the weeds and wild wood of Sin!

Thus, paradoxically, this 're-discovery' of the Green Man has often proved more conducive to the creation of new mythologies than to a better understanding of his real significance.

Some contrasting approaches to the Green Man

Fresh interest in the image has produced a spate of books and articles with fundamentally differing approaches to the topic. Most fall into two main categories. The first of these assumes the existence of an ancient, all-pervading concept or deity, identified as the Green Man, who plays a leading role in practically every belief and custom regarded as traditional.

The idea that the leafy Green Man represents something archetypal and fundamental to all mankind is an attractive one. Indeed, in most ancient cultures and religions, trees and other forms of vegetation are objects of veneration and even worship. Most societies, apart from the seal-hunting ones of the north, depend for survival on vegetation of some kind or other, whether as fodder for cattle or food for humans. All the early civilizations of Asia Minor and the Eastern Mediterranean had among their many gods one or more who originally represented vegetation in general and who came increasingly to represent the corn-seed that was buried in the earth to rise again in the new harvest. Such gods include the Mesopotamian Dumuzi (Tammuz); the Egyptian Osiris, who, originally a nature god, took on the role of the God of the Dead; the Phoenician Adonis, born of a mother who had been transformed into a myrrh-tree; and the Phrygian Attis, whom Cybele turned into a pine-tree.

Pagan religions were generally broad-minded and prepared to show respect for, and even to adopt, gods not originally their own. These would be incorporated into the local pantheon, sometimes under different names and sometimes with additional, newly created myths. The Greeks, for example, had their own corn goddess, Demeter, who was known to the Romans as Ceres (hence cereals), but this did not prevent them from adopting Adonis, the dying and rising Phoenician deity, in whose honour they would plant shards or shallow dishes with fast-growing seeds, which would spring up rapidly and wither equally rapidly. These short-lived 'Adonis Gardens' would be displayed during the Adonia festival, celebrated immediately after the harvest, and they would then be thrown into the sea or some other source of water. Shakespeare and his contemporaries were clearly familiar with this ancient custom, for, in *Henry VI Part 1* (Act I, scene 8), the Dauphin tells Joan of Arc: 'Thy promises are like Adonis' garden, That one day bloomed and fruitful were the next'. Shakespeare refers to the custom in the past tense, but in staunchly Catholic Malta, once colonized by the Phoenicians, it survives to this day in a thin Christian disguise. Each year as Christmas approaches, Maltese children sow wheat and canary-seed in shallow dishes, which are kept in the dark until the seeds sprout. The dishes are then placed near the figure of Baby Jesus in the crib under the Christmas tree.

Trees, as well as corn, have played an important role in cults and customs throughout the ages, and the reasons for this are easy to grasp. Trees are so much larger and stronger than people, and live so much longer. With their roots in the earth and their crowns in the sky, they appear to bridge the three worlds – Lower, Middle and Upper – which figure in many mythologies. Some trees appear to possess the secret of life by remaining green in winter when most vegetation dies back, while others give the same impression by losing their leaves in autumn and becoming green again in spring. Trees provide people with fruit for food, and wood for fires, houses, boats, utensils, and even idols. Trees flourish by essential sources of water. They attract lightning, and they assemble in terrifying large numbers in dark forests where a man may lose his way and be assailed by named and nameless fears and perils.

Folk imagination has peopled these forests with innumerable supernatural beings, such as nymphs, fairies, elves, sprites, goblins and witches, many of whom are essentially malevolent, and most of whom are, at best, capricious and treacherous. The beauty and majesty of trees led people to regard individual specimens, and even

Two foliate heads over the west portal of the church of Notre Dame,
Caudebec-en-Caux, Seine Maritime, Normandy. 1426–1539.
Photo: Ruth Wylie.

whole groves, as sacred. Few who have walked among the great
Redwoods of the United States will think this strange. Even today, in
the twenty-first century, people both plain and sophisticated still
make sure of obtaining suitable greenery for Christmas and other
traditional festivals which require it.

One of the earliest and most influential of a number of
publications belonging to this first category is *Green Man: The
Archetype of our Oneness with the Earth* by William Anderson, with
photographs by Clive Hicks, who later went on to write other books
from a similar standpoint. Anderson's book, which appeared in 1990,
undoubtedly had the effect of bringing foliate heads to the attention
of a wider public, and of turning many readers into Green Man
enthusiasts. However, not all of those who were initially intrigued
and inspired by the book remained wholly satisfied with its approach
and its assumptions. Some felt that, on closer inspection, it contained
too many flights of fancy and failed to make a proper distinction
between proven fact and the author's own personal, subjective
reaction to the image. Not everyone was convinced that the foliate
heads in churches actually represented all that was claimed.

A different approach is adopted by writers such as Kathleen
Basford [*The Green Man*, 1978, reprinted 1996], Mike Harding [*The

Roof boss in vaulted chancel of Holy Cross church, Avening,
Gloucestershire. Photo: Ruth Wylie.

Little Book of the Green Man, 1998], and Jeremy Harte [*The Green Man*, 2001], who are reluctant to venture beyond what can be asserted with reasonable certainty, and who do not set out to create an icon for environmentalists, or gather the maximum number of religious and folkloric phenomena under a single green umbrella. There is wisdom in their wariness. Much progress has, indeed, been made in tracking down and recording examples of Green Men, but our understanding of their significance is still comparatively limited. For this reason, the most reliable and sensible books are often those with the least text and the most illustrations!

The Green Man in Britain by Fran and Geoff Doel (2001) is a cautious book which does not fit neatly into either of the above two categories. Although many of the illustrations are of ecclesiastical carvings and there is a gazetteer of them, only one short chapter is

A foliate head on a corner of the Taverne de l'Ours,
Rue Champeaux, Troyes, Aude, Champagne-Ardennes.
Photo: Ruth Wylie.

specifically devoted to them. The rest explore concepts of greenness, the tale of Sir Gawain and the Green Knight, various folk customs involving flowers and foliage, and some modern interpretations of the Green Man in the arts, without reaching any hard and fast conclusions.

Definite conclusions are, indeed, hard to reach, given the many forms of the motif, spread over so wide an area and so great a time-span. A lot of nonsense has been written about Green Men, much of it imaginative and thus superficially attractive. This has had the effect of leading some enthusiasts into blind alleys, and of preventing them from picking up vital clues.

The present book explores the Green Men found in churches and elsewhere without making any limiting prior assumptions of the kind that all Green Men represent a single archetype or some pagan fertility deity. It aims to dispel some popular misconceptions and to trace the history of the image, as far as it can be ascertained, taking into account the changing character and outlook of the communities which used the motif in their architecture and applied arts.

Some conclusions are reached but failure to find all the answers need not impair our enjoyment of the motif. It certainly did not worry Kathleen Basford, one of the pioneers in the study of the Green Man. Not long before her death, she sent me a letter in which she wrote: 'I have never tried to 'explain' the theme. Indeed, I am happy that the Green Man remains an enigma. Oh, but he is such an opportunist, and full of surprises.'

And so he is! In evolutionary terms, Green Men form an extraordinarily successful species. For centuries, they have survived by colonizing new niches and adapting to changing conditions, and, as we shall see, they are still at it.

2: SOME SUPPOSED ALIASES OF THE GREEN MAN

This chapter will explore some of the figures commonly identified with the Green Man and the foliate heads in churches. Since Lady Raglan first suggested that the Green Man might be connected with certain figures in folklore the list of his possible aliases has grown apace. In one book or another, an amazing assortment of images has been identified with the Green Man. They include ancient deities, such as Tammuz, Osiris, Dionysus, Pan and Cernunnus; semi-historical and wholly legendary figures, such as King Arthur, Robin Hood, the Green Knight, St George, Herne the Hunter, and al-Khidr; and folkloric characters, such as the May King and Queen, Maid Marion, Jack-in-the-Green, Morris dancers, the Castleton Garland, the Wodewose, and a great many more besides.

This line of approach is a hangover from the days when even eminent anthropologists and folklorists were apt to interpret data in terms of some preconceived fixed idea, such as the notion that all folk customs were, at bottom, survivals of ancient fertility rites, or represented the struggle between summer and winter. Sir James Frazer (1853–1941), author of *The Golden Bough* (1890), was probably the most famous of those whose interpretation of valuable data suffered from the prevailing urge to find a single common denominator. After him, others continued to fall into the same trap, although nowadays most folklorists seek to fit the theory to the facts and not vice versa.

During the last two or three decades, much good, scholarly research has been done in the field of traditional British customs and rituals by people who employ the methods and standards accepted in other branches of history. Some oft-repeated myths have been exploded, and some faulty assumptions have been corrected, not least those concerning the antiquity of certain customs.

Many scholarly monographs and articles on individual aspects of British folklore have already been published in journals and as separate works, but those seeking a single volume which will acquaint them with the present state of research on major customs and rituals cannot do better than consult Ronald Hutton's *The Stations of the Sun: A History of the Ritual Year in Britain*, 1996.

Parallels and connections undoubtedly exist in the realms of folklore and religion but, when searching for them, Green Man enthusiasts would do well to take a leaf out of the rule-book of mushroom gatherers. In the world of fungi, superficial resemblances are common, but failure to take note of essential differences can have unfortunate consequences!

Cernunnus, King Arthur and Robin Hood

Green Man 'twinnings' on the scale adopted by some writers bring their own problems, because, if the Green Man can be identified with a number of different images, then it must follow that all these different images are fundamentally the same, and can also be identified with each other. This, however, is clearly not the case.

Some ancient Mesopotamian and Mediterranean deities do, indeed, possess sufficient common characteristics to justify our regarding them as one god under different local names, but this is not the case with other figures sometimes identified with the Green Man. We would, for example, be hard put to say precisely what Cernunnus, King Arthur and Robin Hood had in common.

Robin Hood and the Celtic deity, Cernunnus, certainly shared an interest in deer, but Cernunnus wears the magnificent antlers of a red stag on his head, while Robin sees deer primarily as a source of food. Robin, moreover, is a thoroughly down-to-earth human being, unsuited to the role of a forest spirit. He is a reflection of specific historical circumstances, and represents the voice of those whose ancient rights to gather wood and pasture animals in royal forests were being whittled away by various newcomers in the shape of barons, abbots, sheriffs and other officials. Due to the weakness or impecunity of the monarch, these newcomers were able to acquire land, including forests, and power, which they used unjustly. Far from being the King's enemy, Robin acts as his self-appointed steward, dispensing justice and preserving in the greenwood the traditional features of an ideal realm until such time as they can be officially re-established nationwide. Whether we take the earliest ballads about Robin Hood or the nineteenth-century novel *Ivanhoe*, an important element in the tales is the appearance of the King in the greenwood, where the outlaws entertain him, convince him that right and virtue are on their side, and declare themselves to be his most true and loyal subjects.

In contrast to the Arthurian legends, the traditional ballads and tales about Robin Hood contain nothing that is magical or supernatural. They have no equivalent of Merlin or Excalibur.

Robin's bow was neither made from a magic yew, nor acquired under special circumstances and, intrinsically, it was no different from those issued to the Sheriff of Nottingham's men. Robin was simply a highly skilled archer and fighter, like the bowmen who brought England victory at Agincourt, and he did not always dress in Lincoln green.

The tale of Sir Gawain and the Green Knight

The story of Sir Gawain's strange encounter with the Green Knight has attracted considerable attention from those interested in the Green Man. At first sight, the magical Knight - green-named, green-skinned, and green-clad - may well seem a promising match for the Green Man. Closer inspection of the text will, however, reveal more differences than similarities between them.

This Arthurian adventure does not appear in Sir Thomas Malory's work *Le Morte D'Arthur*, written during the second half of the fifteenth century, and is known only from a poem composed by an unknown author towards the end of the fourteenth century. For those who do not know or have forgotten the details of the tale, I will summarize them here.

The story begins with the unexpected appearance of the Green Knight during the Yuletide celebrations at King Arthur's court. The Knight's clothes, skin, hair, armour and horse are all green - an indication of magic, since green was the fairy colour. Indeed, at the end of the tale, we learn that he is, in fact, an ordinary human knight, Sir Bertilak, who had been temporarily rendered green in appearance by Arthur's often malicious half-sister, the sorceress Morgan le Fay, in pursuit of a plan to make Queen Guinevere die of shock. Unarmed except for a mighty axe, the Green Knight carries a holly branch in his hand as a sign of peace, and requests 'a Christmas game'. This consists of allowing anyone bold enough to take the axe and strike him a single blow, in any way that he pleases, on condition that, a year and a day later, the contender will appear at the Green Chapel to receive a return blow without flinching.

The proposal is greeted with derision and incredulity, and nobody makes a move until Arthur himself rises in response to the Knight's taunting remarks about the company's apparent cowardice. Then Arthur's nephew, Sir Gawain, declares that it is not fitting for the King to accept such a challenge, and volunteers to take his place. Gawain strikes off the Green Knight's head, but, to everybody's astonishment, the stranger survives, picks up his head, which continues to speak calmly, and, holding it by the hair, he rides away.

In the following November, Sir Gawain sets out to seek the Green Chapel, the whereabouts of which are unknown. After much travelling, he finds shelter in a magnificent castle, where he is royally entertained by its lord and lady. His host, whom he does not recognize, is the mysterious Green Knight in his normal, ungreen, state as Sir Bertilak, and he makes a new bargain with his guest: at the end of each day, each will give the other anything that he has received. On three successive days, Sir Bertilak goes out hunting, while Sir Gawain remains in the castle, where his hostess attempts to seduce him. She is, in fact, testing his knightly honour on the instructions of her husband. Sir Gawain successfully resists temptation, and, on the first day, he receives a chaste kiss, followed by two on the second day, and all these he passes on to Sir Bertilak, who hands over his share of the hunting bag. On the third day, however, the lady forces Gawain to accept her green silk girdle as a gift, in addition to a kiss, and asks him to conceal the gift. This he does, thus breaking his word to Sir Bertilak.

In due course, guided by one of Sir Bertilak's retainers, who tries to dissuade him from continuing, Sir Gawain arrives at the Green Chapel – a kind of cave, overgrown with weeds, which strikes him as evil-looking and associated with the Devil. The Green Knight duly appears, with his head once more on his shoulders, and armed with a new Danish axe. Gawain submits to being struck, and the Green Knight makes two feints. Only with the third stroke does he inflict a slight cut on Gawain's neck. The Green Knight now tells Gawain that the cut represents his breach of faith over the girdle, and explains all the other circumstances of the adventure, including his own identity and the role of Morgan le Fay. Sir Gawain is mortified by the stain on his honour, and freely admits his guilt. The two knights part as friends, and Sir Gawain returns to King Arthur's court to tell of his adventures and his shame. The full original text of the poem, together with a prose translation into modern English, Introduction and notes by W.R.J. Barron, can be found in *Sir Gawain and the Green Knight,* 1979.

The central theme of the tale has less to do with greenness than with the code of chivalry, with the shame that results from its least infringement, and with the frailty than can lurk beneath the shining armour of the most faultless knight. All things considered, it is hard, if not impossible, to make any firm connection between Sir Bertilak and the foliate heads which we find in churches. As for the Green Knight, he may be green all over but, apart from the holly branch which he carries when he enters Arthur's hall (but not subsequently),

Sean Connery as the Green Knight in Sword of the Valiant, *1984.*
Copyright Stephen Weeks Collection.

there is nothing leafy about him or his apparel. In any case, holly is virtually unknown among the identifiable leaves of Green Man carvings.

One attempt to link the Green Knight to vegetation offers the suggestion that only a plant can be beheaded and live. However, this ingenious argument appears less convincing when we realize that the strange challenge issued by the Green Knight is not exclusive and unique to him, but represents a recycling of an older legend relating to the Irish hero Cuchulain. Here, the challenge forms the final round in a series of trials involving magic to determine which of the three outstanding warriors of Ulster – Laegaire, Conall Cernach, and Cuchulain – is entitled to the Champion's Portion at feasts. Of the three, only Cuchulain finds the courage to submit to the return blow, which, naturally, does not harm him, and he therefore wins the contest. The unknown challenger then reveals himself to be the very chieftain whom the three rivals had earlier invited to judge between them, and who was skilled in magic.

Al-Khidr – the 'Green One'

Another exotic figure supposed by some to be one of the Green Man's aliases is al-Khidr (more properly al-Khadir), who is a legendary Islamic immortal especially revered by Sufis (Islamic mystics). Muslims identify al-Khidr with the unnamed Servant of Allah who, in the section of the Koran entitled 'The Cave' (Chapter 18), is described as having been endowed with Allah's own mercy and knowledge, and who therefore possesses insight denied to most. The Koran relates how Musa (Moses) makes a journey in the company of al-Khidr, and finds his actions extremely hard to understand or justify. He looks on in amazement while al-Khidr bores a hole in the bottom of a ship, kills a boy, and rebuilds without payment a damaged wall in a city whose inhospitable inhabitants refuse to give them shelter. Musa's questioning of these actions leads to their parting company, but not before al-Khidr has explained how, in each case, he acted at the command of Allah to avert still greater evils.

In the Koran, Musa's strange companion is anonymous, and in no way associated with greenery of any kind. He owes his nickname to later Arab commentators, who embroidered the original story and dubbed him al-Khidr, meaning the 'Green One', because, according to some, he turned green after he had drunk of, or dived into, the Spring of Life – an incident not recorded in the Koran itself. In these later stories he appears as a supernatural being to chosen mortals, who recognize him by his shimmering robes of brilliant green, a colour regarded by Muslims as their own. Indeed a ban on the wearing of green garments was among the many restrictions imposed upon the subject Christian population during the Ottoman occupation of the Balkans.

The mythologies surrounding al-Khidr received further local embellishment in various parts of the Islamic world, where he gained much popularity as a kind of guardian angel or saviour in time of danger. He was also regarded as a saint blessed with special metaphysical insight which enabled him to penetrate the truth beneath appearances and to discover another, more God-like, dimension. In parts of what is now India and Pakistan, he became transformed into Khwadja Khidr, a deity who protects travellers by water. One of the more widespread legends about him tells he turned himself into a log to save a man who had fallen into a river.

Yet despite the greenness of his robes, he too, even more than the Green Knight, lacks the foliage which is an essential feature of Green Men.

Jack-in-the-Green

Much nearer home there is a truly leafy character widely believed to be the incarnation of the Green Man. This is Jack-in-the-Green – a man in a basketwork frame covered with greenery and flowers, who dances during May Day festivities.

Lady Raglan was the first to connect the two in her historic article of 1939. Unfortunately this seemingly plausible theory was disproved by one of the next generation of folklorists, Roy Judge, whose research was first published in 1975 as *The Jack in the Green: A May Day Custom.* He showed that the custom, which is peculiar to chimney sweeps, went no further back than the late eighteenth century.

On the basis of contemporary drawings and descriptions, Roy Judge traced the changes in the dress and practices of the chimney sweeps and other professions which took to the streets on May Day. He found that, up to the middle of the seventeenth century, it was the custom for milkmaids to dance with flower-decked pails on their heads. The fashion then changed and they abandoned their pails for a pyramid of borrowed silver plate (jugs, tankards, platters, etc.), which was known as a Garland although it was mostly metal. During the eighteenth century, some chimney sweeps and bunters (rag-pickers and other women at the bottom of the social scale) took to appearing on the streets on May Day with Garlands of silver plate on their heads, apparently in imitation of the milkmaids. The sweeps had previously dressed up as Lords and Ladies, wearing huge wigs and fine clothing, with their faces whitened with chalk in contrast to their usual layer of soot, and they would bang the brushes and shovels of their trade.

The earliest reference to the inclusion in the sweeps' procession of a Jack-in-the-Green dates from 1795 and describes a leafy, bush-shaped structure which covered the entire bearer, apart from his feet

A contemporary Jack-in-the-Green at the Sweeps' Festival in Rochester, Kent. The Festival was revived in 1983 after a lapse of some eighty years. Photo: Ruth Wylie.

and lower legs. The prime purpose of the sweeps' procession through the streets was to collect money to see them through the summer season when there was less work. Since, more often than not, they would squander the lot on drink, they soon came to be regarded as mere beggars and a sordid public nuisance.

By the middle of the nineteenth century, the custom had virtually died out, but it was later revived in a sanitized form by those nostalgic for a vanished Arcadian Merry England. Roy Judge's investigations suggest that, in its heyday, Jack-in-the-Green was predominantly a London custom which spread to other urban areas, mainly in the south, and especially between London and Oxford.

Unfortunately, this meticulously documented research has not prevented sincere, but ill-informed, enthusiasts from perpetuating an imagined connection between Jack-in-the-Green and the Green Man heads in religious buildings erected long before there were sweeps or even chimneys. Recently, a number of towns and organizations have re-introduced Jacks-in-the-Green into their 'traditional' festivities. No doubt this adds colour to the proceedings, and gives pleasure to both citizens and visitors alike. It is, however, a modern interpretation of a largely imagined ritual, which can add nothing to our understanding of foliate heads.

The *peperuda* in Bulgaria

A person covered from head to foot in foliage and known by a variety of names, including *peperuda*, was once a familiar sight in the villages of Bulgaria and other Balkan countries. The similarity to Jack-in-the-Green is, however, only 'leaf-deep', and this underlines the importance of not jumping to conclusions on the basis of superficial resemblances.

The Bulgarian *peperuda* is always a specially selected young girl, preferably an orphan, and her role is to induce rain during periods of drought. The custom has no fixed date, but is performed as and when necessary. The *peperuda* dances round the village, pausing to allow householders to pour water over her and to offer her entourage gifts of flour, onions and other produce, but never eggs, because these are too suggestive of destructive hailstones! When all the houses in the village have been visited, the *peperuda* goes to the nearest river, where her greenery is taken off and thrown into the water.

The name *peperuda* means 'butterfly' in Bulgarian, and the term may reflect the rapid arm movements of the dance. It has also been suggested that the word is a corruption of the name of Perun, the ancient Slav God of Thunder – and, therefore, of summer rain. The same god is commemorated in the name of the Pirin Mountains in the south-west of Bulgaria, and in the Bulgarian word for 'iris' (perunika), a flower which blooms in the season when thunderstorms are frequent.

While *peperuda* is the most common Bulgarian name for the custom, other words, such as *rosomanka, voidanka, dudola, vay-dudola, vay-gugu* and *oy-lyulé*, are found in some southern and western districts of Bulgaria, and in parts of what is now the Former Yugoslav Republic of Macedonia. *Rosomanka* and *voidanka* are derived from words meaning 'dew' and 'water' respectively, but the origin of the other names has not yet been satisfactorily explained. [MacDermott 1998: 230–2]

The study of folk customs is easier in the Balkans than in England. In most Balkan countries the traditional rural way of life, together with a complete system of folk customs relating to key events in the life of the community and the individual, survived well into the twentieth century. Prior to the Second World War, no upheavals comparable to those caused by the Reformation, Puritanism, and the Industrial Revolution, interrupted the natural evolution of tried and trusted customs. Thus the pioneer ethnographers of the nineteenth century and their more recent successors were not delving for relics of a vanished culture, but recording a living tradition in all its local peculiarities and variations. Fortunately they were recorded! At the end of the Second World War, three-quarters of the population of Bulgaria was still living in villages without paved roads and farming scattered strips of land as their forefathers had done for generations. Industrialization began in earnest during the 1950s, and by the end of the 1970s the majority of the population had moved into rapidly expanding towns and cities to do jobs that were unknown to their parents. Rapid urbanization and other far-reaching social and economic changes soon rendered many folk customs irrelevant. The introduction of large-scale modern farming and the building of dams to provide irrigation put an end to the need for *peperuda*. Numerous other customs disappeared from everyday life, while some survived in a modified form.

The change came about so fast that, unlike their British counterparts, Bulgarian folklorists do not yet have the problem of having to distinguish the genuine tradition from the inventions of well-meaning revivers. When obsolete, discontinued customs are re-enacted for the public at folk festivals, the actors or producers are often elderly people who, in their youth, performed the selfsame customs as part of their everyday life.

A similar situation exists in other recently industrialized Eastern European states. If, in our exploration of Green Men, I seem to favour Bulgarian parallels, this is because I have lived and worked in Bulgaria for many years, and have first hand knowledge of local customs both currently practised and already relegated to the stage.

Foliate heads in religious buildings are extremely rare in Slav countries such as Bulgaria and Russia, which are Eastern Orthodox in religion. Some occur on the exterior of ancient Russian churches built during the twelfth and thirteenth centuries, and further mention of these will be made in a later chapter. In Bulgaria, the motif appears in the great church of the Rila Monastery, on the carved wooden pulpit and altar screen, but these date only from the nineteenth century.

A foliate head quite unlike any other can seen on the altar screen of a side chapel in the Rozhen Monastery, which is situated in south-west Bulgaria, close to the frontier with Greece. The heart-shaped face has thin black moustaches, sparse black hair, and pig-like ears on the top of the head. This face is so constructed that it seems to consist of two profiles, joined by a single broad nose and a wide mouth, which disgorges leaves and huge brightly painted flowers. The screen is believed to date from the sixteenth century.

A foliate head on the altar screen of a side chapel in the Rozhen Monastery, Bulgaria. Photo: Spaska Paskova.

Nobody in Bulgaria appears to have paid any special attention to these foliate heads, and as yet they have no name. Obviously they cannot be connected with the *peperuda*. The only Bulgarian art-historian to venture an opinion said that possibly the Rozhen head represented the Tree of Jesse – a theme to which we shall later return.

The May King and May Festivities

In Britain, May Kings and Queens have a much longer and more respectable pedigree than Jack-in-the-Green, but they, too, have been objects of imaginative speculation. While they have been identified with the Green Man by Lady Raglan and others, they have also been seen as folk memories of a deposed pagan god, and as relics of an ancient fertility rite in which they were sacrificial victims.

These are theories based more on wishful thinking than on real historical evidence. As far as sacrifice is concerned, the timing does not seem right. In May, the cereal crops are already green and sprouting, and require little thought or attention. Recorded customs aimed at ensuring a good harvest tend to coincide with an earlier phase of the agricultural year, namely, ploughing and sowing. This is the case in Britain, where, on Plough Monday (early in January), a plough would be blessed by the parish priest and then decorated and paraded around the village by the local ploughboys. These would collect money to keep 'plough lights' (candles) burning in the church during the vital work of preparing the fields for sowing.

19

The same timing was observed at the opposite end of Europe in Bulgaria. Here the individual farmer would perform a whole string of rituals when preparing to sow his fields. In some districts, the Shrovetide festivities include ritual ploughing, accompanied by a kind of play in which one of the participants represents a 'tsar' who 'dies' and is 'resurrected'. [MacDermott. 1998: 196–7] Fertility rites to encourage the vines to produce an abundant harvest are likewise performed, not when the leaves or grapes appear, but when the bare canes are pruned on February 14 and libations of last year's wine are poured on the soil. This custom is still popular in Bulgaria, and is annually observed by all who have vineyards, however small. [MacDermott 1998: 182–3]

Extremely little is known for sure about the pre-Christian rites of either Celtic or Anglo-Saxon Britain. Some Celtic tribes celebrated May Day under the name of Beltane, which means 'bright fire', and most of the evidence indicates that it was a festival primarily concerned with cattle rather than crops. By the beginning of May, the weather was usually sufficiently warm and the grass sufficiently grown for cattle to be taken further afield, or up into the hills, to graze, and they were driven out between two fires to protect them from evil influences.

Similar ceremonies involving cattle and purifying bonfires still take place in the Carpathian Mountains in Eastern Europe on May 6 (St George's Day according to the old Julian Calendar), when cattle and sheep depart for the high meadows where they are pastured during the summer [Milovsky 1987: 51–9]. In Russia, too, the same date saw ceremonies connected with cattle. There, St George's Day was the traditional date when animals were allowed to graze in the open for the first time after the long, hard winter. Women would drive them out of the farmyards with branches of pussy-willow - a tree believed to have powerful magical qualities for good. As the animals went out, the women would recite charms for high milk yields. Prayers would be said to St George, whom the Slav peasantry regarded first and foremost as a protector of cattle, even though the Church usually portrayed him as a knight on a white horse, slaying a dragon. He was also thought to send down the first dew of the year, and Russian peasants would roll in the dewy grass for their own health and welfare [Rozhnova 1992: 84]. The vital importance of the reappearance of succulent fresh grazing is reflected in the old Russian name for the month of May – *Traven* – which means 'grassy'. April was known as *Snegogon* – 'snow-chaser'.

In Bulgaria, St George's Day (known as *Gergyovden* and also celebrated on May 6) has livestock in the form of sheep as the focal point of the numerous customs associated with this festival. The ewes are milked for the first time, and lambs are ritually slaughtered and eaten at communal feasts in the open air. In a modified form, these customs are still widely observed, especially by shepherds, and even urban families do their best to get a whole lamb for lunch on *Gergyovden* [MacDermott 1998: 214–24].

The return of warmer weather and the greater availability of animal products, such as milk, cheese and fresh meat, is celebrated all over Europe with customs which often have much in common, and are clearly ancient. Milk, for example, forms a link between the Bulgarian celebration of St George's Day and the English milkmaids' processions on May Day, In both countries, too, the festivities begin with a mass exodus into the meadows and woods to fetch greenery, with young people spending the night or early hours of the morning out in the countryside, and with all and sundry bathing or rolling in the dew. There are also certain differences. Russia and Bulgaria, for example, have no Maypole or May King and Queen. In England and Bulgaria, the climate permits farmers to plough and sow their fields long before the Maytime festivities, but in Russia this work has to be done *after* St George's Day, so that May can be a very hectic month in regions where spring comes late.

In mediaeval Britain, the improved weather and the lull between seed time and haymaking allowed the country folk to organize events known by various names, such as the May Games. These would consist of all kinds of pleasant activities, including feasting, dancing, singing, pageants, sporting events and plays [Hutton 1996: 244–61]. The clergy did not always look with approval on such pastimes, but by the fifteenth century the games were used to raise funds for the village churches. Often the festivities included the election and crowning of a mock king or queen to preside over the events. This, however, was not always the case, and the 'king' was an additional attraction, rather than an essential feature of the games.

During the fifteenth century some Scottish towns elected mock 'Abbots' with fanciful names, such as the 'Abbot of Unreason' or the 'Abbot of Bon Accord', to preside over their early summer revels. These 'Abbots' performed a role similar to that of the Lords of Misrule who organized the Christmas festivities in royal and aristocratic residences [Hutton 1996: 249].

In Tudor times the vogue for plays about Robin Hood led to people dressing up as the famous outlaw and his Merry Men, and joining in the pageants and processions as well as, or instead of, the May King.

If any connection existed between the May King and the Green Man carvings in churches, we would expect the revellers to pay some kind of attention to them at some point in the proceedings. There is, however, absolutely no evidence of foliate heads ever being the focus of open or furtive public attention during the May Day revels or, indeed, at any other time. Some churches appear to have been closed during the games, but for much the same reasons as Eros in Piccadilly is boarded up as a precautionary measure at times of modern national rejoicing. Those who voiced criticism of the games did so either because they thought that they encouraged immorality and unseemly behaviour, or because they were afraid, especially after the Peasants' Revolt of 1381, that large gatherings in the open air might lead to insurrection.

Contemporary descriptions, both factual and in fiction (such as Malory's account of Queen Guinivere's Maying in *Le Morte D'Arthur*), portray 'bringing in the May' simply as an enjoyable festive excursion into the woods in the company of friends (and lovers - hence fears of immorality). There is nothing to suggest that either the participants or onlookers saw the May King and his entourage as anything more than gorgeously attired carnival figures. This is borne out by those sources which describe Robert the Bruce, newly crowned King of Scotland, as resembling 'a Summer King' or 'a King of Summer'. They cannot have meant that he was dressed as a forest deity, or kitted out with leaves and branches like one of Malcolm's soldiers advancing on Dunsinane! (Luyard 1890 iii:130 and Robbins 1959: 16; cited in Hutton 1996: 247)

By now some readers may be thinking: 'This chapter has got us no nearer to finding out who the Green Man is.' To some extent this is true, but the elimination of suspects and the investigation of false trails has always formed part of a detective's work, and the same holds good for exploring Green Men. Having cleared the ground a little, we shall be able to make greater progress towards the truth.

3: THE GOTHIC REVIVAL

Those who are curious about the real origin and meaning of the Green Man will, by now, be aware of the pitfalls and dead ends involved in trying to assimilate a variety of images into a single entity. A net spread too widely may catch so many red herrings that the truth may slip through unnoticed!

Instead of pursuing the maximum of possible 'green' connections, we should concentrate on the specific characteristics of the mysterious foliate heads, paying due attention to the historical circumstances of time and place.

In this chapter we shall begin a journey of exploration, tracking the Green Man back towards his origins. Our route will resemble an archaeological dig in that we shall start by examining the 'layers' closest to the present. We shall then work our way back through the major stylistic periods, including Italianate, Gothic and Romanesque, until we unearth the earliest images of the Green Man.

Two key questions for explorers

As we delve into the past, we shall be searching for answers to two questions that are crucial to solving the 'riddle' of the Green Man. The first question concerns the precise identity of the pagan god whom he is thought to represent.

Like Christian saints, most pagan deities are usually portrayed with certain features and attributes which make them instantly recognizable to devotees, and to archeologists and art historians. Pallas Athene with her helmet, Gorgon-decorated shield and Little Owl; Ganesha with his elephant's head, rat companion and handful of sweets; Kali with her black face, protruding tongue and necklace of skulls; Dionysus with his wreath of vineleaves, grapes or ivy, and his *thyrsos* topped with a fir-cone; Horus with his falcon's head; Thor with his hammer; Zeus with his eagle and thunderbolt; Pan with his reed pipes and goat's legs, ears and horns; Mithras with his Phrygian cap and bull – all these are familiar to most of us.

If, however, you do not know what to look for, you may not be able to distinguish between, say, Shiva and Vishnu, or Ra and Osiris. To the uninitiated all Indian deities tend to look alike and the same could also be said of Green Men. The latter all have foliage of some kind, just as all Indian gods have more than one pair of arms. But, despite their many arms, Shiva and Vishnu differ in origin, attributes

A Victorian misericord in the church of St Peter, Wintringham, North Yorkshire. The misericord was designed by Temple Moore and carved by James Elwell in 1889.
Photo: Ruth Wylie.

and mythology, and most Hindus concentrate their devotion on either one or the other.

Could Green Men with leaf-mask faces be different in origin and significance to those who disgorge vegetation? Until we know, we would be wise to explore 'Green Men' rather than 'the Green Man', and to be prepared to find the trail running in more than one direction. To do otherwise would be to assume too much too early.

The second key question follows on from the first: if the Green Men represent pagan deities, how can we account for the apparent absence of any objection on the part of the Church hierarchy or individual Christians to their presence in Christian buildings?

Devotees of Sherlock Holmes will recall the 'curious incident of the dog in the night time', which, to the great detective, was significant precisely because the dog did nothing in the night time. An analogous and equally significant non-event occurs in the history of the Green Man. At the present time theories and claims about Green Men abound, but, if we step back into the past, whether a few decades or several centuries, there is silence. The Green Men are there, all right, multiplying and mutating, but nobody makes any comment or displays any curiosity about their meaning and origin. Why?

*A foliate head on the chancel arch of the church of St Michael,
Aston Tirrold, Oxfordshire. The date on the head is 1852.
Photo: Ruth Wylie.*

We will now begin our journey of exploration in the most recent
period when, as it were, Green Men were seen but not heard, namely
in Sherlock Holmes's own Victorian age.

The Victorian background

The God-fearing Victorians clearly had no doubts about the
respectability of Green Men. They energetically restored them in
existing churches, lovingly fashioned new ones for the churches built
to accommodate the expanding urban population, and extended
their habitat to include business premises and secular public
buildings.

Theirs was the age when iron and steam transformed Britain from a largely agricultural country into the industr)al centre of a world-wide Empire. In the process, both wealth and squalor were created on an unprecedented scale. Manufacturing towns and cities acquired imposing civic centres, with solidly built banks, exchanges and emporia, surrounded by a dingy jungle of slums and grimy factories.

The technical and scientific advances of the Victorian age were not always paralleled by architecture that was as revolutionary in appearance as the Crystal Palace. On the contrary, when the arbiters of public taste grew bored with eighteenth-century classicism, they looked to the more distant past for inspiration. Isolated examples of a renewed interest in Gothic had appeared during the late eighteenth century, but in Victorian times this trickle became a mainstream flood.

Among the pioneers of the Gothic Revival were members of the Oxford Movement, formed in 1833 by Anglican clergy who wanted to resurrect certain Catholic doctrines and rituals that had been discarded during the Reformation. Their reintroduction required changes in the layout and furnishing of churches. By then, most of the old fear and animosity felt by Anglicans for the Catholic Church had evaporated, and the Catholic Emancipation act of 1829 had lifted the remaining restrictions on those who still adhered to Catholicism.

The most famous of the professional architects who supported the revival of Gothic for secular as well as ecclesiastical buildings is Augustus Welby Northmore Pugin (1812–52), who was a Catholic convert. As well as making designs, he wrote books offering philosophical and moral arguments in favour of the Gothic style.

Similarly high-minded, intellectual support for Gothic came from the critic, artist and social reformer John Ruskin (1819–1900), who was the first man in England to be appointed Professor of Art. His beautifully written books (especially *The Seven Lamps of Architecture* and *The Stones of Venice*) were immensely influential, and he introduced a new note by concentrating his attention on Continental Gothic. Gothic architecture also found favour with the Pre-Raphaelite Brotherhood, and with William Morris (1834–95) and his circle.

Ruskin had been brought up in a strictly Evangelical tradition and, indeed, enthusiasm for the Gothic Revival was found right across the religious spectrum, and even among the irreligious. William Morris, for example, had originally intended to enter the

A pair of nineteenth-century foliate heads on the stepped gable of a mansion in the Esplanade Park in Metz, Lorraine, France.
Photo: Ruth Wylie.

Anglican Church. He lost his religion but not his admiration for Gothic architecture and certain other aspects of the Middle Ages.

For Morris the attraction lay in the creativity and independence enjoyed by the mediaeval craftsman and denied to the factory worker. He was not opposed to machinery and modern inventions as such, but deplored the shoddiness and poor taste of mass-produced goods.

The Victorians' fondness for Gothic was not always as backwards-looking as it might seem at first glance. The engineering used to construct Gothic-style buildings was often the very latest that the Industrial Revolution had made possible. William Morris's love of beauty and craftsmanship led him to seek not merely new designs in furnishings, but a new form of society. In later life he became an active Socialist, writing militant songs and speaking on soap-boxes at street corners.

Victorian Green Men

Victorian buildings provide an excellent hunting-ground for Green Man spotters. The architects who copied the pointed arches, towers and spires of glorious mediaeval churches also copied, in their own

way, many of the minor decorative elements that went with them, including foliate heads of various kinds. They reproduced these elements on houses and public buildings as well as on churches.

A number of Green Men appear on the Houses of Parliament, designed by Charles Barry (1795–1860) and Augustus Pugin. Several are easily visible around the entrance under the Victoria Tower. After the old Palace of Westminster was destroyed by fire in 1834, the powers-that-be stipulated that it should be rebuilt in either Gothic or Elizabethan style. Barry's own preference was for Italianate architecture, and the young Pugin assisted him to draw up the prize-winning design and to make the finished building sufficiently Gothic in detail to please the traditionalists who were to sit in it.

One of the best places to see Victorian Green Men is Lancing College in West Sussex. The magnificent chapel, breathtakingly high, in French Gothic style, was designed by R.C. Carpenter in the middle of the nineteenth century. An enormous number of Green Men can be found on the richly carved choir stalls. The Chapel is regularly open to the public.

A fine colony of Victorian Green Men reside in the centre of Birmingham, most of them on secular buildings, with two on St Philip's Cathedral and one on St Chad's. Twenty-three of Birmingham's Green Men are listed, with illustrations and a map, in a convenient booklet written by Anthony Hayward [*The Green Men of Birmingham,* 2002].

So what can the Green Men of the Victorian age tell us about the meaning and origin of the image? Unfortunately, practically nothing.

Foliate heads as such were not discussed by any of the gurus of the Gothic Revival. Not even by the prolific Ruskin, who described the Nature of Gothic in such wonderful English prose, and who actively encouraged the young ladies of Whitelands College in London to celebrate May Day according to a 'tradition' devised by himself. He personally designed costumes and jewellery for the students' May Queens, but his imagination did not stretch to including Green Men in the proceedings. Ruskin was just one of

Opposite: *One of the many Green Men on the choirstalls of Lancing College Chapel, Sussex. The Chapel is in early French Gothic style and the foundation stone was laid in 1868. The stalls, designed by Walter Tower, and their canopies, designed by Gilbert Scott, were presented to Lancing by Eton College. Photo: Ruth Wylie. Reproduced by kind permission of the Friends of Lancing College.*

many enthusiastic Victorian revivers of 'traditions'. None of them attempted to link foliate heads with folk customs, either genuine or imagined.

We must conclude that, for the Victorians, foliate heads were simply part and parcel of the Gothic style. Any message that they may have carried for mediaeval worshippers had been lost during the intervening centuries. They were regarded as a traditional decorative motif, which was to be enjoyed and exploited, but which did not require analysis.

We, too, may enjoy the ubiquitous Victorian Green Men, but they can tell us no secrets, because none was embodied in them. To learn more we must continue our journey back into the past.

4: FROM THE RENAISSANCE TO ROMANTICISM

Between the Gothic Revival and the genuine article which inspired it lay several centuries of growth and upheaval. During this time, people's ideas, attitudes and way of life underwent so many radical changes that little, other than the enduring stones of surviving Gothic churches, remained the same.

Green Men continued to appear, but, like everything else, they assumed new forms and different roles. If our object is not simply to discover Green Men, but to try and make sense of them, then dates and contexts are of paramount importance. So, before exploring the Green Men of this long and exciting period, we shall look briefly at the salient features of the historical and cultural background.

The Renaissance

During the fourteenth and fifteenth centuries, Western Europe began to experience a complete transformation of the ways in which people thought, acted and viewed the world in which they lived. This process became known as the Renaissance (meaning 'rebirth') – a reference to the rediscovery and revival of the classical heritage of Greece and Rome. This, however, was only one aspect of the Renaissance as a whole, which both arose from and gave rise to a wide range of economic, political, social and cultural changes.

Although English and several other European languages, including Russian, adopted the French for 'rebirth', the Renaissance actually began in Italy, in the city states ruled by the middle classes. These newly emerged classes had values and aspirations that were different from those of the mediaeval knights and clerics who had dominated society during the age of Gothic. They no longer saw the material world as an unavoidable 'Vale of Tears' – a kind of dark, uncongenial corridor through which one made one's way to the blissful Life Beyond, practising austerity and self-denial, as advocated by the Church, in order to avoid ending up in Hell. Their paramount virtues were those necessary to succeed in business, such as thrift, industriousness, and pride in craftsmanship, and they boldly asserted Man's right to happiness and pleasure on Earth as well as in Heaven.

31

A sixteenth-century grandfather clock in the Cathedral of Saint-Cyr and Sainte-Julitte, Nevers, Nièvre, Burgundy. Photo: Ruth Wylie.

Despite being people of action rather than contemplation, they were bursting with fresh ideas. These they embodied in a new philosophical system, known as 'humanism' because it shifted the centre of attention from God to Man as an individual. In retrospect, we can recognize that the humanist ideas of the Renaissance contained the seeds of future secularization, but this would not have been apparent to those who formulated these ideas, nor was it their intention.

Renaissance humanists were neither irreligious nor agnostic. They saw the world as a heavenly creation, essentially beautiful and harmonious, and they sought to discover and comprehend the laws governing this heavenly harmony. Observation and exploration of the world and the individual were central to the aspirations and activities of the Renaissance humanist. People were recognized to be complicated, many-sided creatures, and individuals were encouraged to develop in as many directions as possible. Those who sought prominence strove to combine scholarship with public

A leaf-mask and other foliate heads on a sixteenth-century screen in the south aisle of the church of St Michael, Marwood, Devon. Photo: Ruth Wylie.

service, and the ideal Renaissance Man was one with encyclopaedic interests and abilities, who was equally competent as a statesman and a poet, as a warrior and an intellectual. Thus, the Renaissance brought not only the revival and utilization of the achievements of the classical world, but also the proliferation of experiments and discoveries in numerous other fields, including literature, art, architecture, natural history, anatomy, astronomy, mechanics and geography. Politically, it saw the emergence of national states and absolute monarchies.

Italy then had far more surviving relics of Roman buildings than it has today, so Renaissance architects had no lack of models to inspire their churches, palaces and civic buildings. Pediments, rectangular windows, round arches, friezes, balustrades, and columns and pilasters with capitals of various classical orders, were some of the salient features of their work.

The circle was widely regarded as the most harmonious and perfect of forms, so many of the new churches were round or polygonal in shape, with a huge dome (representing the Universe) over a central altar. Churches in the form of a square or a Greek cross (one with four equal arms) were also popular at this time. For some, the innovations were too extreme, and they adopted the dome while retaining the nave. In many northern countries, the new style found expression in the addition of fashionable classical elements to existing churches in local style, rather than entire new buildings.

The Reformation

During the sixteenth century, certain aspects of the Renaissance combined to fuel the Reformation and the spread of Protestantism. These aspects included the importance given to the individual, the excessive pursuit of worldly pleasures by the higher clergy, and even the Popes, and the invention of printing, which made books, among them the Bible, available to far more people than had ever previously been possible.

In Germany pressure for reform of the Church came from below, with Martin Luther's protests against the sale of Indulgences in 1517. Theoretically, Indulgences permitted people to buy remission of punishment on Earth or in Purgatory for their sins but, in reality, their sale funded the upper clergy's extravagant life style.

In contrast England's Reformation began at the top, with Henry VIII's quarrel with the Pope (1533–4), and with the Dissolution of the Monasteries (1536–9) to the benefit of the Crown and nobility, but Protestantism gained ground and popularity during the reign of Elizabeth I (1558–1603), though not without some violent suppression of Catholicism.

Protestants rejected the supremacy of the Papacy, accepted the Bible as the only source of truth, and believed that individuals could be saved only through their own faith. In the eyes of Protestants, priests were not authorized to forgive sins; neither could saints nor the Virgin Mary act as mediators between individuals and their God. Some more extreme Protestants, such as the Puritans, went much further than the Church of England in their desire to simplify church ritual and dispose of all the trappings of Rome. During the period of the English Civil War (1642–9) especially, there was wholesale destruction of images of saints and the Virgin Mary, stained-glass windows, and anything else that smacked of 'Popery' in churches and cathedrals throughout the country.

The Counter-Reformation

Faced by the serious challenge to its teaching posed by the expansion of rational sciences, by growing criticism, and even by loss of power

A panel on the Fontaine d'Amboise in the park in Clermont-Ferrand, Puy de Dôme, Auvergne. 1515. The seed capsules are poppy-heads. Photo: Ruth Wylie.

in some European states, the Catholic Church embarked on a Counter-Reformation, in a determined effort to reform itself.

Numerous theological definitions and measures to meet the crisis were debated and agreed at the sessions of the Nineteenth Ecumenical Council of the Roman Catholic Church (the 'Council of Trent'), which took place in Trento (northern Italy) between 1545 and 1563. The Society of Jesus, usually known as the Jesuits, was founded in 1543 as an organization of Roman Catholic priests devoted to educational and missionary work.

The dramatically ornate style of architecture known as Baroque, which developed during the seventeenth century, was closely associated with the Counter-Reformation, and reflected the Catholic Church's desire to impress and overwhelm worshippers emotionally, so that there would be no room in their minds for dissident thoughts.

Adapted to secular use, as in Louis XIV's palace complex at Versailles, the grand scale and flamboyant opulence of Baroque art and architecture aimed to express the absolute power of the monarch in the same way as it expressed that of the Roman Catholic Church in an ecclesiastical setting.

Interestingly enough, the term 'Baroque' was, like 'Gothic', originally used pejoratively, and it was derived from a Portuguese word denoting a 'misshapen pearl' by those who regarded the style as a distortion of the harmonious simplicity of early Renaissance

*The back panel of a choirstall in the Cathedral in Sées, Orne,
Normandy. Photo: Ruth Wylie.*

architecture. Even at the time, some felt that Baroque had gone 'over the top', and during the early part of the eighteenth century, a new style known as 'Rococo' came into fashion. If still complicated, it was lighter and more delicate. The term 'Rococo' was derived from the French word *rocaille,* meaning 'loose pebbles', and refers to the shells and pebble-like shapes which, together with twining flowers and vines, were typical elements of the style. Although it originated in Paris some of the finest examples of Rococo as applied to ecclesiastical buildings are to be found in Germany and Austria.

The Enlightenment

England had accomplished her bourgeois revolution in the seventeenth century, with the victory of Parliament and the middle classes over absolutism and the establishment of a constitutional monarchy. In France and elsewhere, however, absolutism continued to flourish and the middle classes, despite their growing economic importance, remained excluded from political life and power.

The years leading up to the American and French Revolutions at the end of the eighteenth century saw the development of a philosophical trend known as the Enlightenment, or Age of Reason, whose representatives in many countries were formulating new, democratic ideas, based on a rational, scientific approach to a wide range of issues, such as education and the State. These ideas included opposition to all vestiges of feudalism and absolutism, hostility towards religion which used superstition to enslave men's minds, and an optimistic belief in human progress.

The architecture of the eighteenth and early nineteenth centuries was characterized by a return to classicism, which found its main expression not in churches, but in secular and public buildings, such as museums, theatres, libraries and seats of government.

Romanticism

During the late eighteenth and early nineteenth centuries, Romanticism appeared as a reaction to classicism and philosophical rationalism. In literature, art and music, the Romantics rejected classical restraint and reason in favour of emotion, imagination, and a belief in the innate goodness of human beings, and the need to return to unspoilt nature. Romanticism was also characterized by admiration for the heroic individual and a fascination with all things exotic, such as the East and the Middle Ages.

There was also an increased interest in folklore and ancient religions. One of the earliest phenomena to attract attention was Druidism, about which little is known even today apart from what Roman authors, such as Caesar, recorded. John Aubrey (1626–97) was the first to suggest that Stonehenge, whose true age was then unknown, had been built by the Druids. This idea was taken up in the 1740s by the antiquarian William Stukeley, who, carried away by his own romantic fantasies, extended them to other ancient monuments as well. His enthusiasm was contagious and, during the eighteenth and nineteenth centuries, Neo-Druidic orders were established on historically dubious foundations, which, however, proved lasting, since 'Druids' still appear at Welsh Eisteddfods, and at Stonehenge for the summer solstice! Neo-Druidism was the first of many 'revivals' characteristic of the nineteenth and twentieth centuries.

Gardens during the Renaissance and after

As part of our preparation to explore Green Men we should equip ourselves with at least a general understanding of how people related to plants and nature during the period under examination.

Botany was among the many subjects scientifically investigated by inquisitive men of the Renaissance, who founded the first botanic gardens where medicinal herbs and rare plants were carefully studied and classified. Voyages of exploration and the establishment of better communications with distant lands brought all kinds of new plants into Europe.

The period of the Renaissance was one of relative peace and prosperity, so that the rich no longer felt the need to live in fortified castles or to restrict their gardens to tiny enclosed plots. Italians with the money to do so emulated the classical philosophers and public figures who, like Pliny the Younger, sought tranquility in rural retreats, where artistic and intellectual activity could flourish away from the noise and bustle of the towns. The first such country villas were, indeed, fairly modest and secluded but, inevitably, as time passed, they became grander and grander, until they were less of a rural sanctuary and more of a means of impressing visitors!

Among the pioneers of Renaissance country villas were members of the Medici family, which, though obscure in origin, had acquired immense wealth and power through commerce and banking. Probably the most magnificent Renaissance garden of all is that of the Villa d'Este, created between 1550 and 1580 for Cardinal Ippoliti II d'Este, a scion of an ancient noble family which had ruled

Leaf-mask with cornucopiae emerging from the eyes. On a panel screening a side chapel in the Church of the Trinity, Fécamp, Seine Maritime, Normandy. Commissioned by Antoine Bohrer, 25th Abbot (1507–19). Photo: Ruth Wylie.

Ferrara and Modena since the thirteenth century. The site of the Villa d'Este, to the east of Rome, is appropriately close to where the Emperor Hadrian (117–138) once commissioned a comparable establishment, and relics from the Emperor's villa were removed and recycled by the Cardinal.

Classical statuary, greenery, topiary (a feature of ancient Roman gardens), mazes with low hedges, grottoes, fountains, cascades and other elaborate contrivances using water, and rising terrain with panoramic views over the surrounding countryside, even though the gardens were walled, constituted important elements of the Renaissance rural retreat. No actual Roman gardens had survived, so the garden-makers of the Renaissance found inspiration and guidance in the works of classical authors, such as Pliny and Ovid, which they interpreted in their own way.

In the flatter, more heavily forested land of France, two of whose sixteenth-century kings, Henri II and Henri IV, married brides from the Medici family, Renaissance gardens were less vertically designed than those of Italy. The sunny hills of Italy, with their cypresses, olive trees and vines, provided suitable vistas. Even their wild thickets could be incorporated into the corners and edges of the more unpredictable and dramatic Baroque creations, but the darker, thicker forests of France still seemed threatening, untamed and uncongenial, and they had to be excluded from gardens altogether.

Typical of the French version of the Renaissance were the huge, rigorously ordered geometric *parterres*, resembling carpets or embroideries, created by André le Nôtre (1613–1700) at Vaux-le-Vicomte, and brought to a dazzling climax at the Palace of Versailles (begun in 1665).

To all intents and purposes, Versailles was conceived as the temple of the 'Sun King', Louis XIV (1643–1715), with ubiquitous allusions to Apollo, the Sun God, and his sister, Diana, Goddess of the Hunt. Hunting was a sport passionately enjoyed by the Bourbon monarchs of France. Everything at Versailles was designed to reflect the power and glory of the absolute King, who embodied the State in his own person, who required even the vegetable kingdom to obey his will and every whim, and who, according to the Duc de Saint-Simon, 'took superb pleasure in compelling nature'.

Elements of Italian and French gardens spread to many other countries through travellers, royal marriages and books. Elizabethan England favoured the knot-garden, which consists of intricate symmetrical patterns formed from lines of low, neatly clipped

A panel on the tomb of Thomas James, Bishop of Dol, in the Cathedral of St-Samson, Dol-de-Bretagne, Ille et Vilaine, Brittany. Sixteenth century. The work of two Florentine sculptors, Antoine and Jean Juste. Photo: Ruth Wylie.

greenery, such as box or thyme, enclosing flowers or herbs. During the seventeenth century, English gardens became bigger and more ambitious, but they remained walled enclosures formally planted, where cultivated nature was never confused with the wild nature of the countryside beyond.

By the middle of the seventeenth century, however, a new vision of unspoilt nature was encouraged by the works of artists such as Nicola Poussin (1594–1665) and Claude Lorrain (1600–82), who painted exquisite Italian landscapes which evoked a past Golden Age.

The dream of Arcadia – a rustic paradise, where it was always summer, and where carefree shepherds and shepherdesses had nothing more arduous to do than join nymphs and sundry sylvan deities in making music and love – was not a new one. Arcadia was, in fact, a real historical place – a region of ancient Greece famed for its flocks and herds, and seen by classical writers in nostalgic, idyllic light, thus tempting Renaissance writers and poets to do the same.

By the eighteenth century, some people were tiring of the excessive formality and order that characterized Renaissance garden style and were ready for a change. In England, 'Capability' Brown (1716–83) pioneered the landscape garden, uprooting knots and *parterres* to bring green meadows, lakes and naturally shaped trees right up to the windows of great houses, with only an invisible ha-ha to keep the deer and cattle out. The fact that Brown's 'natural' landscapes, with their bodies of water, temples, and clusters of trees, were every bit as meticulously planned and engineered as le Nôtre's formal vistas in no way dismayed his clients, who were satisfied that their estates had been transformed into something approaching Arcadia.

Not everybody approved of 'Capability' Brown's transformations. One critic is supposed to have said to him: 'Mr Brown, I very sincerely desire that I may die before you.''Why so?' enquired Brown. 'Because I should like to see Heaven before you had improved it.'

By the time that the Gothic Revival was in full swing, the Industrial Revolution had dispelled dreams of a pastoral Utopia. Mass displays of flowers were once again fashionable in gardens large and small, and in the public parks that graced Victorian cities.

Green Men 'reborn'

For many Green Man enthusiasts, the flamboyant, sometimes startling, Green Men of the Gothic period form the star attraction,

A carving in the choir of the Cathedral, Córdoba, Spain. Eighteenth century. Photo: Mercia MacDermott.

with the result that other periods tend to receive less attention. This is a pity, because much can be discovered both in the intermediary period which we are now exploring and in the earlier Romanesque age.

Much more work needs to be done in recording and analyzing the foliate heads of the Renaissance and subsequent eras, but certain changes in location and design are readily discernable, together with a tendency towards what is unquestionably a purely decorative role.

As we shall see when we reach the next chapter, the earlier Gothic form of architecture had provided plenty of opportunities for Green Men to be incorporated into roof-bosses and the capitals of pillars. These traditional Green Man habitats were lost with the change to Classical forms of architecture. Roof-bosses became unnecessary and capitals were carved in imitation of Greek and Roman models, and masons could no longer give free rein to their imagination. However, as if to compensate for this, foliate heads began appearing in secular and domestic settings which provide exciting new hunting grounds for both spotters and explorers.

Following the Renaissance the grotesque, often disturbing, Green Men of the Middle Ages went out of fashion, and the new disgorgers were more stylized in form, and less prone to be oppressed and stifled by their foliage. The latter frequently takes the form of decorative swags, or intricate arabesques, or even drapery, all of which the heads seem not so much to be disgorging as simply holding in their mouths.

In general, disgorging heads, or ones with facial features that sprout foliage, are far less common than they were in Gothic times. There are, of course, exceptions, among them the fine disgorging heads on the Baroque woodwork of the Catholic cathedral built in the middle of the great Mosque in Córdoba.

The geometric leaf-mask, which fits conveniently into triangular and rhomboid spaces, as well as on corners, continues to be popular, which is not surprising, since its ancestry stretches back into classical times.

In Italy – birthplace of the Renaissance, and a country which had previously shown comparatively little interest in foliate heads – the most ubiquitous form of the Green Men is the type which we shall dub 'Italianate'. This has a roughly bell-shaped head, and the foliage is concentrated around the lower part of the face to form a short well-kempt, frill-like beard, which curls outwards and upwards on either side. Such heads may also have foliate moustaches and eyebrows – a style which may be traced back to ancient Rome.

In classical times, such heads represented the Titan Okeanos, one of the older generation of Greek deities, who were eventually ousted by the Olympians. The name Okeanos was also given to the great River Ocean, which, the ancient Greeks believed, surrounded the whole world. The Titan Okeanos married his sister, Tethys, and from the union were born three thousand daughters – the Okeanid nymphs, and three thousand sons – all the rivers and springs. After Zeus and the Olympians had defeated both the Titans and the Giants, Poseidon – usually depicted with a trident – became the dominant water-deity, and Okeanos departed into distant retirement, although he continued to be a popular subject for decorative art, if not for temple-dedication and worship. He is usually portrayed with a beard formed of seaweed, and his horns of power take the form of crab's claws. Sea creatures may be entwined in his hair and beard, and sometimes his face also bears traces of seaweed.

Easily recognizable with his marine beard and crab's claws, Okeanos can still be seen in the House of the Vetti in Pompeii, as a

A Roman mosaic of Neptune, with the seaweed beard and hair characteristic of his predecessor, Okeanos. From a tessellated pavement discovered near the village of Maiden Newton, and now in the Dorset County Museum, Dorchester. Photo: Ruth Wylie. Reproduced by courtesy of Dorset County Museum.

repetitive design on the walls around the peristyle garden, while in Herculaneum he appears, flanked by winged beasts with curling foliate hindquarters, over the arch of an alcove in the inner courtyard of the House of Neptune and Amphitrite.

Seaweed is easily transformed into terrestrial foliage, and a similar motif, with a short curving leafy beard, minus claws, but with large ears, and a foliate cap or crown, frequently appears in Italian art of the fifteenth and sixteenth centuries, such as altar-pieces, tombs, fountains, and the borders of illuminated manuscripts. Heads of this kind can also be seen around a portrait of the Madonna and Child (Santa Maria di Osri Merios) in Seville Cathedral.

Other types of foliate motifs popular during the Renaissance include half-figures rising out of plants, heads surrounded by arabesques of stems and foliage, and animals and birds shown in profile with curling vegetation instead of hind legs and tails. Even the legs of angels have been transformed into coiling tendrils on a wrought-iron grille in Seville Cathedral!

All these are adaptations of Roman prototypes which tourists can see in Pompeii and Herculaneum. Similar examples would have been visible, if less well preserved, on Roman ruins all over Renaissance Italy. Some of the heads may represent Okeanos, or Bacchus, or even the latter's drunken companion, Silenus, but most appear to have been anonymous, purely ornamental figures.

*Two foliate figures on the frontispiece (architectural gateway)
in the Fellows Quadrangle, Merton College, Oxford. The
frontispiece was completed in 1610.*
*Photo: Mercia MacDermott. Reproduced by kind permission of
The Warden and Fellows of Merton College, Oxford.*

Explorers do not have to go all the way to Italy to see examples of the 'reborn' Roman Green Man. The galleries of the Victoria and Albert Museum in London contain numerous examples of Italian applied art, including plaster casts of objects still in Italy. So many of the exhibits are ornamented with foliate heads that a visit to the Museum can prove a real treasure-hunt for Green Man explorers!

There is, for example, an altar-piece from Florence (dated c.1493–97) by Andrea Ferrucci, with a typical 'Italianate' Green Man, wearing a kind of hat or crown, surrounded by coiling stems, two of which develop into burning torches, encircling a central motif with ears of barley.

A variant of the Renaissance Green Man which gained permanent popularity in Spain consists of a coil of vegetation with a figure or head (animal, bird, or human) at either end. This type of design appears, for example, on a wrought-iron screen above the doors of Seville's sixteenth-century *Ayuntamiento*, or Town Hall, where several more foliate heads, both human and animal, can be

Twentieth-century tiles in the Plaza de España, Seville.
Photo: Mercia MacDermott.

seen carved in stone on the highly decorated, plateresque-style façade. Some four centuries later, similar motifs were used to great effect in coloured tiles in the Plaza de España, constructed for the Ibero-American Exhibition held in Seville during 1929.

The same type of motif occurs in a German setting in a picture painted by Lucas Cranach the Elder (1472–1553) for the base of an altar-piece for the town church in Wittenburg. Here the artist shows his friend, Martin Luther, preaching from a pulpit decorated with a carving of a foliate boar's head, whose leafy 'tail' coils round to end in a tiny human head. Cranach had contacts with humanist circles and was an enthusiastic supporter of the Reformation.

Green Men on tombs and memorials

Although foliate heads lost ground as architectural elements during and following the Renaissance, they gained popularity as motifs on tombs and memorial tablets.

Of particular interest, in view of the royal connection, are those in the Capilla de los Reyes (Royal Chapel) in Granada, Spain. The chapel was commissioned at the beginning of the sixteenth century by that most pious royal couple, the Catholic Monarchs Ferdinand and Isabella, to house their own tombs. Here many foliate images

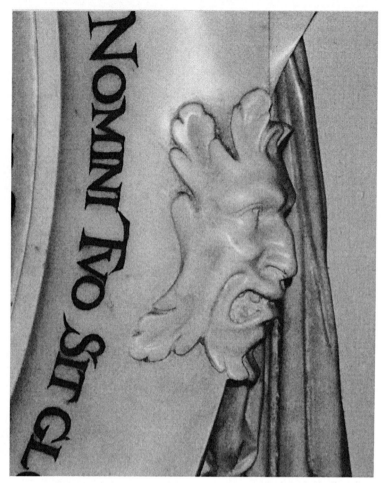

*A foliate head on the memorial to John Bankes (died 1644) in
Christ Church Cathedral, Oxford. Photo: Mercia MacDermott.
Reproduced by kind permission of the Dean and Chapter of
Christ Church Cathedral, Oxford.*

can be seen. On the sacristy door there is a head emitting greenery.
Leaf-masks form part of the decoration on the tombs of the Catholic
Monarchs themselves, and also on those of their daughter, Joan the
Mad, and her husband, Philip the Handsome.

In Italy, too, they appear on the tombs of the high and mighty,
such as Pope Julius II, in Rome, and Lorenzo and Giuliano de'
Medici, in the Medici Chapel in Florence, which were the work of
Michelangelo himself.

A Green Man appears on the frieze at the base of Cardinal Ascania Sforza's highly ornate, sixteenth century tomb in the church of Santa Maria del Populo in Rome. A plaster cast of this can be seen in the Victoria and Albert Museum.

In Britain, too, there are many examples of Green Men decorating the tombs of worthies who died during the sixteenth and seventeenth centuries. Several can be seen on the lavishly carved tomb of Anthony Harvy (died 1564) in the north choir aisle of Exeter Cathedral. Here, in addition to family crests and coats-of-arms, and a cockle shell, one can see a large foliate head, prominently set in a quatrefoil on the front panel of the tomb itself, as well as a disgorging head, and several foliate figures, both human and animal, in the coiling branches which decorate the arch of the canopy above.

Harvy's tomb is largely mediaeval in design and appearance, but the change to a new style is obvious in the slightly later tomb of Sir Willia [sic] Gerrarde in Chester Cathedral. This gentleman died in 1581, having held a number of public posts, including that of Recorder of Chester. The tablet above his tomb resembles a classical portal with an arch between two pillars with Ionic capitals, and on it there are no less than four foliate heads, centrally placed one above the other, on the arch, architrave and frieze, and just below the coat of arms which surmounts the whole.

The memory of Edward Cole, thrice Mayor of Winchester, who died in 1617, is perpetuated in the city's cathedral by a monument in the shape of a portal or window, with many classical features, including an arch, side pillars and pilasters, all lavishly ornamented, painted in several colours and additionally gilded. The structure rests on three corbels, on each of which there is a carved head with a leafy neck and hair. There are three gilded leaf-masks on the base of each of the pillars flanking the arch, and, on the frieze between them, two more heads hold festoons of ribbons in their mouths.

John Bankes, who died in 1644 and was buried in Oxford Cathedral, is commemorated by a fine marble tablet, carved with cherubs' heads, drapery, swags and various convoluted scrolls. On either side of the memorial inscription (flanked by the words *Non nobis, Domine, non nobis, sed nomini Tuo sit gloria* – 'Not to us, O Lord, not to us, but to Thy name be glory') is a leaf-mask with the corners of its mouth turned down in the style of a tragic theatrical mask.

All these grand tombs and memorials are inside churches but, in many parts of Scotland, tombstones with Green Men on them can be seen in churchyards and cemeteries, including Greyfriars, in

*A disgorging head on an eighteenth-century tablestone in Tranent
kirkyard, East Lothian. Photo: Ruth Wylie.*

Edinburgh, and Tranent, East Lothian. Burials inside churches were
forbidden there in 1560, following the Reformation, and all new
churches were of the simplest design, without 'Popish' carving.
Masons were, however, permitted to exercise their skill on
tombstones, and many of them are elaborately carved with various
edifying and consoling Christian symbols.

Green Men started to appear on Scottish tombstones during the
seventeenth century and achieved their greatest popularity during the
eighteenth century, at the end of which they apparently became less

A disgorging head on an upright eighteenth-century gravestone in Tranent kirkyard, East Lothian. Photo: Ruth Wylie.

fashionable. Scottish Green Men are extremely varied in design, and some were clearly inspired by carvings in ancient churches. One finds, for example, some 'cat-faced' Green Men – a style typical of Romanesque architecture, and abandoned in Gothic times.

Betty Willsher has made a special study of Scottish tombstones, and some of her findings in relation to Green Men (which she, too, prefers to call 'foliate heads') were published, together with a gazetteer, in an article entitled 'The Green Man' in the *Scottish Local History Journal* (Willsher 1996).

Secular and domestic Green Men

One of the most striking results of the Renaissance as it affected Green Men was their migration out of the churches into the secular world. Deprived of their traditional homes on roof-bosses, capitals, misericords and choir-stalls by changes in architectural fashion and Protestant insistence on unadorned simplicity, foliate heads re-appeared in all manner of secular settings from lintels to door-knockers.

The examples given in this section are just a taste to whet your appetite for what can be discovered once you learn to look out for Green Men in streets, museums, antique shops, stately homes, gardens, Mediterranean holiday resorts, and just about everywhere, instead of just in churches.

Aberdeen's Mercat Cross is another striking example of how Scottish masons found a secular outlet for skills that were no longer required in churches. Built in 1686 with funds provided by local guilds, the Cross is of the type that consists of a smallish open-sided structure designed to provide shelter for merchants and market-goers. The richly carved stonework includes such an astonishingly high concentration of foliate heads of various kinds that no single photograph could give an adequate impression of the whole.

Well-heads are among the items that were often decorated with 'Italianate' Green Men. Fine specimens can be seen in the gardens at Kingston Lacy (Dorset), Stansted Park (Hampshire), and Sandringham (Norfolk).

Italian wall-fountains also often have foliate heads, and two can been seen in the Victoria and Albert Museum. One is an elaborate affair from Florence, dating from the first quarter of the sixteenth century and consisting of an alcove within a highly decorated door-like frame, which is ornamented with birds, shells, twirling foliage and two 'Italianate' heads. The other fountain, made in Verona during the second half of the sixteenth century, has at its corners ferocious-looking beasts, which disgorge foliage ending in smaller heads of a similar kind.

The same museum has two Italian chimney-pieces displaying foliate heads. The first is a marble original, made in Milan during the late sixteenth century. It is richly decorated with numerous 'Italianate' heads, figures of Pan, vegetation, and other motifs, in coloured marble inlay. The second is a plaster cast of one made in Lombardy during the first half of the sixteenth century. It is ornamented with carved coils of vegetation beginning and ending with heads and half-figures. A third chimney-piece, of similar date,

An Italianate head on a well-head in the garden of Sandringham, Norfolk. Photo: Mercia MacDermott.

but from Florence, is decorated in classical Roman style with winged horses whose tails and hindquarters have been replaced by leafy arabesques.

An elaborate English fireplace and overmantle of the 1590s with numerous foliate heads, both human and animal, can still be seen *in situ* in the drawing room at Canons Ashby (Northamptonshire).

A large Italianate Green Man, surmounted by the salamander emblem of the French King François I (1515–47), embellishes the ornate apex of a French dormer window (thought to be from the Chateau de Chambord), once again in the Victoria and Albert Museum.

A much less glamorous situation is occupied by a mid-sixteenth-century English Green Man at Wilton House, Wiltshire, seat of the Earl of Pembroke. Here, a leaf-mask, with a resigned but proud stare, guards the top of a lead drainpipe on the Tudor section of the house. It is visible from the windows of the corridors known as the Upper Cloisters. Early eighteenth-century drainpipes decorated with leaf-masks can also be seen on the west front of Canons Ashby.

Early examples of the domestic use of typically Classical foliate motifs can be found at Powis Castle (Powys, Wales), in the Long Gallery completed in 1593. Here foliate heads, full face and in profile, and beasts with long tails, modelled in plaster and reminiscent of the kind then popular in Seville, form part of the decoration. Less ambitious, but clearly indicative of a desire to introduce into one's own home elements of the latest Renaissance fashion, are the foliate heads at Little Moreton Hall in Cheshire – a quintessential 'black and white' Tudor house, creaking, crooked and apparently kept standing by faith alone! The Hall is surrounded by a moat, which visitors cross to enter the cobbled inner courtyard through a late sixteenth-century gatehouse. On either side of the inner door there are vertical friezes of weathered wood, carved with various motifs, including foliate heads in profile.

An unusual foliate head with a long thin beard decorates another timber frame gatehouse, this time at Stokesay Castle in Shropshire. Stokesay is, in fact, not a castle at all but a fortified and moated manor house, built during the thirteenth century by a leading wool merchant from nearby Ludlow. The present gatehouse replaced an earlier stone one and dates from the late sixteenth or early seventeenth century. The Green Man head can be seen on the north-west corner-post of the gatehouse, within the courtyard.

The inspiration for this strange carved head remains a mystery, but, like those at Little Moreton Hall, he may represent a determination to keep up with the Joneses in respect of Italian fashion. A similar head, with a long beard composed of pairs of leaves, decorates the leg of a marble bench in a bath-house at Herculaneum. The bench-leg is shaped like a human leg with two feet, and the head is situated just below the knee, with the beard running right down to the ankles. Neither Pompeii nor Herculaneum

A sixteenth-century French dormer window, decorated with a foliate head and the salamander emblem of François I (1515–47). Copyright Victoria and Albert Picture Library.

had been excavated at the time when the Stokesay corner-post was carved, but Romans in other cities could have had similar benches which may have come to the attention of those eager to embrace Classical modes.

Foliate heads were extremely fashionable in Jacobean England. There is one, for example, on the wall of the inner courtyard of Blickling Hall (Norfolk), one of the country's great Jacobean houses, built at the beginning of the seventeenth century.

Several leaf-masks, copied from engravings made by Hans Leifrink about 1555–57, look down from the magnificent strapwork ceiling of the dining-room in Aston Hall (Birmingham), built between 1618 and 1635 by Sir Thomas Holte. On the Great Stairs of the same mansion there are creatures with long coiling tails, carved in oak. In the Long Gallery there is a foliate head on the lower border of a tapestry woven in the Paris workshop of François de la Planche and Marc du Coman between 1607 and 1627.

Foliate heads also occur on some English tapestries woven at Mortlake during the seventeenth century. Examples can be seen at Boughton House, Northamptonshire home of the Dukes of Buccleuch and Queensberry. A former owner of Boughton House – Ralph, 1st Duke of Montagu (died 1709) also owned the Mortlake works.

One of the best hunting-grounds for explorers in search of Jacobean domestic Green Men is Knole, in Kent. Reputed to be a calendar house with seven courtyards, twelve entrances, fifty-two staircases and three hundred and sixty-five rooms, Knole's interior decoration offers a commensurate number of Green Men. I gave up counting after recording more than fifty: on panelling, plaster work, grisaille painting up the Grand Staircase, a chimney-piece made of marble and alabaster, pilasters in window recesses, and the frames of pictures.

The first 'green' picture-frame that I noticed was at Ham House, where two leafy faces 'attend' a portrait of Charles I by Vandyke, or a member of his studio. Since then I have examined the frames as well as the pictures inside! At the National Gallery in London, a visit to a temporary exhibition entitled 'Fabric of Vision' yielded two clues to the history of the Renaissance Green Man. A painting by El Greco of 'Christ driving the traders from the Temple' (c.1600) had a frame

Opposite: *Carving on the gatehouse of Stokesay Castle, Shropshire.*
Late sixteenth or early seventeenth century.
Photo: Mercia MacDermott.

decorated all over with golden foliate half-figures and winged animals, with coils and arabesques of foliage in Classical Roman style. Even more striking was the frame of Tintoretto's 'St George and the Dragon' (c.1560). Corinthian columns formed its vertical sides, and, in the middle of the bottom section, a Green Man emitted curls of vegetation which turned into cornucopiae, out of which more vegetation coiled. What was particularly unusual about this Green Man was everything flowed not from his mouth, but from his eyes.

Foliage bursting from the eyes occurs in a few of the more revolting Green Men of the Gothic age, but this is the only non-Gothic specimen that I have so far encountered. This Renaissance Green Man does not, however, shock. He appears serene and untroubled, as though he were simply reminding us of the joy and spiritual riches to be gained by looking at great art. We shall be returning to this head in Chapter 7, because it may be able to shed some light on the mysterious Green Man on the tomb of St Abre in Poitiers, hitherto thought to be unique.

Domestic furniture is another place where foliate heads were employed as decoration during the Renaissance and after. They appear, for example, on some ornate black and gold chairs, made in Venice about 1590, and now in the Victoria and Albert Museum. While these Venetian heads are human in aspect, snarling animal heads were popular as decoration on massive seventeenth-century English furniture, such as chairs and sideboards. A friend of mine owns an impressive Jacobean sideboard, whose elaborate carved decoration includes both disgorging lion-heads and a Green Man showing his tongue. When I saw the sideboard for the first time, my friend was still unaware of the many theories and controversies surrounding foliate heads. Her understanding of the face with the protruding tongue was that it represented a warning against gossiping at table – an interpretation which may well have been in the minds of some seventeenth-century diners.

During the eighteenth century furniture became lighter in style, and, in the picture gallery at Temple Newsam, Yorkshire (a large part-Tudor, part-Jacobean house) visitors can see a pair of Japanese

Opposite above: *A chair-back with a foliate head of the kind that became popular in the seventeenth century. This example is nineteenth-century French, probably from Brittany.*
Copyright Stephen Weeks Collection.
Opposite below: A sixteenth-century Venetian chair.
Copyright Victoria and Albert Picture Library.

A foliate head by Jean Tijou on the ornamental screen of the Privy Garden at Hampton Court. Photo: Mercia MacDermott.

lacquer cabinets (c.1690) which stand on English frames (c.1730) with cabriole legs, claw-and-ball feet, and leaf-masks at each corner.

Among the other Green Men which I have spotted in odd domestic situations is one forming the door-knocker on the front entrance of Blenheim Palace.

At the end of the seventeenth century, the Green Man made a courtly entrance into the English garden in the form of gilded leaf-masks on the ornamental iron screen which separated the Privy Garden at Hampton Court from the river and the populace. The garden was laid out to complement the adjacent royal apartments, rebuilt for William (1689–1702) and Mary (1689–94) by Sir Christopher Wren. The screen was the work of the French blacksmith Jean Tijou, who also made the choir screens, decorated with foliage and leaf-masks, for Wren's great masterpiece – St Paul's Cathedral.

London society followed Italian fashion and the royal example by commissioning foliate heads for the façades of their new town houses, such as those in Queen Anne's Gate, built at the beginning of the eighteenth century.

Green Men abroad

Green Man enthusiasts are accustomed to searching high and low in churches for the objects of their desire, and that is fine, provided that they are interested only in Romanesque and Gothic specimens. Where the Green Men of the Renaissance and later are concerned, the field is much wider and, wherever you may be, there is a possibility of finding a Green Man. I recall, for example, looking out of my hotel window in Malaga, on my first night in Spain, and being greeted by two Green Men, each disgorging neat coils of Classical-style foliage above the lintel of a window across the street (Molina Larib). Much the same thing happened in Granada, only this time the Green Man – part of an elaborate lintel – was 'Italianate', and the coils of foliage were the tails of birds, which ended in secondary heads. In Granada, too, while visiting the Alhambra, I noticed foliate heads on iron rings fixed to the wall of the Palace of Charles V (sixteenth century). Even from the window of the coach in which we were travelling through Spain, I caught sight of foliate heads on various buildings, including an eighteenth-century convent in Jerez and a house in Ecija. The village of Güejar Sierra, near Granada, has an outdoor basin with water flowing from spouts set in what appeared to be very worn foliate heads. Most visitors to Seville walk through the picturesque quarter of Santa Cruz. There, a house on the Plaza Alfaro has an ancient door (probably dating from the seventeenth century) decorated with a number of grotesque heads, and topped by a lintel with a foliate head, disgorging stems ending in one human and one bird-like head.

Malta is another good place for Green Man spotters. Casual strolls through the streets of towns, such as Valetta, Mdina and Rabat, will reveal foliate heads over doors and windows, and on fountains. There are even sixteenth-century organ pipes and parts decorated with foliate heads on view in the Cathedral Museum in Mdina.

I have mentioned the Victoria and Albert Museum on several occasions, but many museums hold pleasant surprises for those interested in Green Men. In the Goya Museum in the French town of Castres, for example, there is an extremely ornate ivory helmet, associated with the British King George II (1722–60). In addition to the British Royal coat of arms on the front, and a winged dragon as a crest, it has two leaf-masks in profile on either side. During the War of the Austrian Succession, George II did, in fact, lead his troops into battle personally, and was the last British monarch to do so, but this magnificent helmet can scarcely have been intended for active service.

The Archangel Michael torments a rich man's soul. Fresco in the narthex of the great church, Rila Monastery, Bulgaria. 1848. Photo by Ivo Hadzhimishev.

Foliate heads did not feature on the Green Knight's armour, but they can be seen on helmets, breastplates and greaves, mostly in works of art, influenced, perhaps by Classical statues of Pallas Athene. A late example is the nineteenth-century bust of Caligula, attributed to Angelo Minghetti, in the Victoria and Albert Museum.

William Anderson [Anderson and Hicks 1990: 128] noted a foliate head on a carving of St Michael in the choirstalls of St Bertrand de Comminges (Pyrenees), completed in 1535. It takes the form of a rhomboid leaf-mask on the boot or greave protecting the saint's left knee. His left foot is placed firmly on a diminutive and rather pathetic Devil with a foliate head.

In the West, St Michael is usually portrayed triumphing over the Devil, but in Eastern Orthodox icons, he is usually shown half-length with a raised naked sword. Sometimes, as in a fresco in Bulgaria's Rila Monastery, the sword is used to torment the soul of an expiring rich man. I have not had the opportunity to study Russian or Greek icons of the saint, but in the Bulgarian examples which I have seen his armour is usually decorated with one or more ornamental heads.

In a Bulgarian icon dating from the late sixteenth or early seventeenth century (now in the collection of the National Art Gallery in Sofia), St Michael has what art historians have described as a 'Medusa head' on his breastplate. It is not, in fact, particularly 'snaky', but consists of a round face with Roman-style coiled tendrils to either side. By the middle of the nineteenth century, when the Ottoman authorities had lifted restrictions on the building of Christian churches, thus creating a need for many new icons, the faces on St Michael's armour had evolved into jawless heads disgorging strap-like fringes. These usually form part of the shoulder-pieces or sleeve of the armour. Such heads also occasionally occur on the armour of other warrior saints, such as St George and St Mina.

The Wild Man or Woodwose

Before completing our exploration of this period by drawing some conclusions from what we know about Renaissance Green Men, we need to give some attention to another popular figure, who, confusingly, was sometimes known as the 'Green Man'.

Although the term 'Green Man' as applied to foliate heads is relatively modern, it was sometimes used in earlier centuries to describe another image: the Woodwose, Woodhouse, or Wildman of the Woods - a shaggy creature, brandishing a club, who, in churches and cathedrals, is generally to be found on misericords, and who, at times, featured in certain types of procession and entertainment.

The name 'Woodwose' was derived from the Old English *wudu wasa* – a 'woodland being', and the idea of 'wildness' entered through the influence of the Middle English 'wood' (*wod*), which signified 'mad' or 'furious'. 'Woodhouse' is a corruption or misreading of 'woodwose'.

The concept of a shaggy, half-human creature which lives with the beasts in the wilderness – desert or forest – can be found in the mythologies and literature of many peoples. In the Assyro-Babylonian epic of *Gilgamesh*, which dates back to the second millennium BC, the hero fights and then makes friends with Enkidu – a hairy being, who had previously lived with the wild animals in the desert. In Greek and Roman mythology, there are fauns, satyrs, centaurs, and the Great God Pan – all of whom are shaggy and part-man, part-beast. Classical writers, such as Herodotus and Pliny the Elder, wrote of strange beings – half-ape, half-human – which were said to inhabit forests and distant parts of the world. Even today, public fondness for the idea that mysterious hirsute creatures still survive in remote regions lingers on in tales of 'Big Foot' and the 'Abominable Snowman', or *Yeti*. Classical representations of Hercules, clad in the skin of the Nemean Lion and carrying his club, may also have influenced the appearance of the Woodwose.

The various Wild Men were generally thought to have a dual nature. On the one hand, they were savage, lustful and uncivilized. On the other, they possessed a natural innocence, which could be turned to good account and transform them into loyal friends and protectors.

In Tudor and Stuart England, Wild Men, dressed either in skins or garments sewn with leaves, were a popular feature in pageants and processions. In the course of an elaborate entertainment offered to Queen Elizabeth I during a visit to Kenilworth Castle, a poet clad in moss and ivy emerged from a wood to compliment the Queen with a suitably loyal address.

Men dressed as Wild Men often acted as 'Whifflers' – people who marched at the head of civic and other processions to clear a way through the crowds. The leaf-clad ones were often referred to as 'Green Men'. This has led one researcher [Centerwall 1977 25–33] to suggest that the pageant 'Green Men' were representations of the Green Man of church architecture, and that Lady Raglan had, in fact, unwittingly hit upon the correct name. However, not all 'Whifflers' were thus attired. Indeed, in Norwich, whose cathedral boasts a fine Woodwose misericord as well as some Green-Man ones, the local 'Whifflers' were quite different in appearance.

An early eighteenth-century account of the procession which traditionally accompanied the election of a new Mayor of Norwich describes the dress of the 'Whifflers' as being scarlet satin breeches, white satin jerkins and hats decorated with a cockade of feathers and ribbons. Moreover, they carried swords, not cudgels, and were

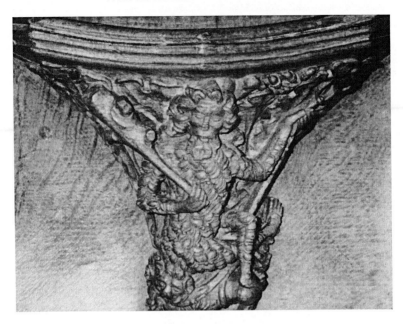

A woodwose on a misericord in Norwich Cathedral.
Photo: Mercia MacDermott. Reproduced by kind permission
of the Chapter of Norwich Cathedral.

assisted by the 'Dick Fools', who wore painted canvas coats with red and yellow cloth caps, adorned with fox or cats' tails and small bells. They were also accompanied by the famous Norwich 'Snapdragon' a fearsome creature made of wood and basket-work covered with painted canvas, with moveable jaws and wings, carried by a man, and associated with the celebration of St George's Day organized by the Norwich Guild of St George, founded in 1385. The Norwich mayoral processions were, however, not entirely without their 'green' aspect, for, on the day of the ceremony, the street where the new Mayor lived would be strewn with rushes and planted with trees [Mackerell 1852].

During Tudor and Stuart times, the terms 'Wild Man', 'Savage' and 'Green Man' were interchangeable, and when, during the seventeenth century, the Distillers' Company took as its heraldic arms the 'Green Man and Still', the supporters took the form of club-bearing shaggy figures. Transferred to inn signs, they tended to be known as 'Green Men', but when Wild Men and Green Men ceased to appear in masques and processions, the relevant inns renewed their signs with pictures of foresters or Robin Hood. Quite recently some have adopted the foliate head.

The connection of foliage with intoxicating liquor is ancient. Ivy was sacred to Bacchus, since it was believed to counteract the ill effects of alcohol. The custom of displaying ivy, or some other greenery, outside premises with wine to sell goes back to Classical times. The saying 'Good wine needs no bush' was known to Shakespeare (*As You Like It* – Epilogue), and to the Romans, who said *Vino vendibili hedera non opus est* (Saleable wine needs no ivy), and passed the saying on to France, where they say *Au vin qui se vend bien, il ne faut point de lierre* (A wine which sells well needs no ivy). In other words, you do not need to advertise a good product!

One possible reason for the Distillers' choice of emblem is because green herbs were then widely used in the preparation of certain popular beverages and, consequently, it was appropriate to depict a herbalist (or 'green man') standing beside his apparatus.

Distillers and publicans were, however, not the only people to use Wild Men and Green Men as their symbols. A naked but shaggy Wild Man and a similar Wild Woman, both crowned with leaves, act as supporters in a representation of the Royal Arms of Sweden dated 1541. In this case, the man holds a cudgel which appears to have vestiges of roots still attached to it. The weapon is represented even more clearly as an uprooted tree on a Brunswick *taler* issued in 1578. This coin depicts a shaggy Wild Man holding a burning light and a small tree with the jagged remains of broken roots and branches. Wild Men and Green Men, bearded, but otherwise smooth-skinned, and wearing garlands of leaves on their heads and about their loins, were popular as supporters for the Arms of several German aristocratic and royal families, including the Kings of Prussia (from 1701 onwards), the Dukes of Pomerania, the Counts and Princes of Schwarzburg (Thuringia), and the Holzhausen family of Frankfurt, as well as the Dukes of Brunswick.[Neubecker and Little 1997].

The popularity of Wild Men and Green Men in German heraldry can be explained by the growth of German national consciousness during the sixteenth century. Patriotic Germans drew on descriptions by Roman authors, such as Tacitus, of the forest-living Germanic tribes who resisted conquest by Rome, and who, under Arminius (Hermann), annihilated a Roman army led by Publius Quintilius Varus in the Teutoburg Forest in 9 AD. The ancient contrast between the sophisticated, but often effete and corrupt, Roman world and the healthier, more virtuous forest-dwellers was fully exploited by German nationalists of the sixteenth and subsequent centuries, who

Modern Green Man pub signs.
Top left: *Hurst, Berkshire.* Top right: *Rackheath, Norfolk.*
Bottom left: *Shatterling, Kent. Photos: Ruth Wylie*

did not see why the Latin races should have all the admiration and be regarded as the model for everybody else. The forest, with its mighty oak trees, became an essential symbol of German national identity and pride; Simon Schama has described this process in detail in his book *Landscape and Memory* (1996: 75–134).

In addition to the usages listed above, the term 'Green Man' has also been applied historically to people in charge of firework displays (in the seventeenth century), to inexperienced sailors, and to the wild orchid *Aceras anthropophorum*. Nowhere and at at no time was there any suggestion of a link between these diverse usages and the foliate heads found in churches and elsewhere.

Some conclusions

If we turn to literature in the hope of discovering the meaning of the various foliate heads and figures which appear in so many contexts in post-Renaissance Europe, we shall draw a blank. There was no lack of books during this period. The prevailing mood of curiosity and enquiry, coupled with the invention of printing, ensured an abundance of writing of every kind from poetry to scholarly study. Yet, unless we are prepared to see a possible coded reference to the Green Man in every mention of trees or the colour green – and there is no good reason why we should – it appears that no contemporary considered the motif sufficiently important to merit mention.

We must therefore rely on circumstantial evidence and our own good judgement.

The Italianate Green Man did not figure in mediaeval churches, but made its appearance – or, rather, reappearance – at the time of the Renaissance as one of the many motifs borrowed from ancient Rome and used decoratively, without any deep significance. The people of the Renaissance and later, who filled their poetry, plays, paintings, gardens, and so forth, with Classical images and allusions, remained solidly Christian, whether Catholic or Protestant, and neither worshipped the ancient gods whom they resurrected, nor believed in the existence of nymphs, satyrs, cherubs and the rest, although they revelled in portraying them.

The use of foliate heads to decorate garden urns, well-heads and fountains, and its extension to wrought iron gates, is a perfectly logical adaptation of Roman precedents.

The frequent occurrence of foliate heads over, or flanking, domestic doorways and windows, suggests that some people may have regarded them as auspicious or protective, as well as decorative. The same may be true of foliate heads on armour, although we must stress that in neither case is there direct evidence that this is so. The urge to protect openings of all kinds against the intrusion of unspecified, unseen evil is both ancient and widespread. Ethnographers consider, for example, that the lavish embroidery at the neck, sleeve edges and bottom hem of Bulgarian folk costumes was originally intended as much to ward off evil as to decorate. It is the unadorned opening which is vulnerable, and the foliate head is just one of many forms of decoration used to remedy the situation by people who may well no longer be aware of the original reason for the custom.

Whatever messages foliate heads may have carried, they were clearly non-controversial, arousing no passions and offending no one. A Green Man, breathing out foliage and cornucupiae filled with leaves and fruit, appears on the decorative border of the title page of Martin Luther's appeal to a General Council (Wittenburg, 1520). The Puritans who took hammers to carvings of the Virgin and the Saints saw no great harm in Green Men and let them be. In staunchly Catholic Spain and Malta, as in Protestant England, Green Men were tolerated in churches and allowed to proliferate in homes and public places. In Italy, where the Renaissance resurrected Green Men and gave them a new lease of life, they appeared in situations both sacred and profane, including a seventeenth-century wine-cooler (Scacchi's frigidarium, 1622), which has prominent leaf-masks above its legs. [illustration, David 1996: 23] Their despondent expression does not, however, encourage the idea that they represent Bacchus. Rather they seem to be ornamental stereotypes, suitable to fill any bare corner.

Much the same type of leaf-mask appears on the memorial to John Bankes (died 1644) in Oxford Cathedral. Here the down-turned corners of the mouth may be intended to emphasize the tragedy of death (see photo page 48).

Tombs and memorials are among the few sites where it is possible to arrive at an accurate interpretation of the original messages conveyed by the Green Men set upon them. Greenery of any description generally expresses the idea of remembrance and renewal. Those foliate heads, and even skulls, which disgorge leaves may symbolize the passage of the immortal soul from the body to eternal life. Foliate heads may also be intended to remind the beholder of one or more of the numerous Biblical references to vegetation in connection with the brevity and transient character of life on Earth, such as 'all flesh is grass' (Isaiah 40.6), or 'there is hope of a tree, if it be cut down, that it will sprout again... but man dieth and wasteth away' (Job 14:7–10). We may be certain, however, that whatever particular idea was in the minds of those who chose to include a foliate head among the symbols on the tombs and memorials of those whom they had loved or respected, the image undoubtedly conveyed a Christian message.

An interesting tomb which combines coarsely grotesque foliate heads with fashionable Classical allusion is that of Richard Harford and his wife (1578), in Holy Trinity Church, Bosbury, Herefordshire. This is adorned by two large human heads, with wide mouths and rows of fearsome teeth, disgorging sprigs of pomegranates split to show the seeds. The pomegranate found its way into Tudor applied art during the reign of Henry VIII, since it was the emblem of Catherine of Aragon. At Ightham Mote (Kent), for example, it occurs in several places, including the painted wooden ceiling of the chapel, together with the Tudor Rose, in celebration of the King's marriage. To the ancients, however, the pomegranate was associated with the legend of Persephone and her sojourn in the Underworld, and it can be found in Roman tomb paintings dating from the fourth century BC, and preserved in the museum at Paestum in Italy. It was adopted into Christian art as a symbol of the resurrection, and sometimes the Christ Child is shown holding a pomegranate, as in Botticelli's 'Madonna of the Magnificat' (in the Uffici, Florence). A pomegranate also makes a symbolic appearance in the basket of fruit on the table of 'The Supper at Emmaus' by Caravaggio (National Gallery, London). Thus, the Green Men watching over the mortal remains of the Harfords in Herefordshire – a part of the world not suited to pomegranate growing – could well indicate a desire on the part of the couple to be seen as up-to-date people with a knowledge of the Classics.

From the information at our disposal, the most logical conclusion is that, in the wake of the Renaissance, Green Men survived and flourished mainly because of their Classical connections and decorative potential, aided and abetted by fashion.

We have traced the ancestry of some Green Men back to Roman prototypes, but the Classical foliate head does not disgorge foliage. The lineage of those Green Men who do must be sought elsewhere. In pursuit of their pedigree, we will now go still further back into the past – to the Gothic 'Golden Age' of disgorging Green Men.

5: THE GOTHIC AGE AND ITS GREEN MEN

Gothic architecture flourished in the Catholic countries of Europe from the middle of the twelfth century to the end of the fifteenth. Despite its name, it has nothing to do with the Goths – a Germanic people who played a leading role in the downfall of the Roman Empire. The term 'Gothic' as applied to architecture was unknown to those who built the great Gothic cathedrals. Like Baroque, it was originally a pejorative word, and was first used by Renaissance Italians who disliked the style and considered it 'crude' and 'barbarous'. Foremost among them was the sixteenth-century art-historian and architect, Giorgio Vasari, who chose to believe that 'Gothic' forms had been introduced to Italy by the barbarians who sacked Rome. Many of his fellow-countrymen were equally unenthusiastic about Gothic architecture, and in Italy it never achieved the universal popularity that it did in France, Germany and England.

The essence and origin of Gothic style

The most obvious and best-known feature of Gothic architecture is the pointed arch. This was not merely a change of aesthetic fashion from the previously ubiquitous round arch. It was also a technical innovation which opened up a whole new range of architectural possibilities.

Pointed arches exert less lateral thrust than round ones, and, in the form of rib-vaulting, they can also bridge wider and more varied spaces than the Romanesque barrel vaults. Strengthened by external flying buttresses, ribs function as a skeleton, supporting the weight of the building, so that the structural role of the walls is minimized. Solid blank stone can be replaced by huge windows. Mediaeval craftsmen were not able to produce large sheets of glass but they made a virtue out of necessity by filling window space with small pieces of stained or painted glass. These were held in place by lead framing and formed beautiful patterns or depicted scenes from the Scriptures. Thus colour, light and airiness of a kind impossible in earlier buildings became the hallmark of Gothic architecture.

Contrary to Italian prejudice Gothic architecture was not a barbarian import but developed in what was then one of the most civilized parts of Europe – the Ile de France around Paris. The region was the power base of the Capet dynasty, named after Hugh Capet, who became king in 987, after the last Carolingian monarch had died childless. The Capetians reunited the country, and set in motion the process which made twelfth-century Paris an international centre of culture and learning. There learned men like Peter Abelard (1079–1142) taught and debated. The first Chancellor of Oxford University, Robert Grosseteste (1175–1255) travelled from England to study in Paris.

Louis VI (1108–37) consolidated his realm and his own royal authority by successfully combatting external enemies and suppressing banditry on the part of local barons. He was also a generous benefactor of the Church, and took as his close adviser Suger, Abbot of St Denis (1081–1151). St Denis is the patron saint of France, and the abbey had been founded as a royal mausoleum by King Clovis in 507. In Suger's time it was still being used as such, although it had become somewhat dilapidated and needed extensive work.

Suger was a learned and energetic man, who held strong views on the role that architecture could play in strengthening faith and piety. He believed in the power of vast, awe-inspiring churches, with forests of columns and soaring arches, with glowing, jewel-like windows telling stories of the Saviour and His Saints, and with every stick and stone gilded, enamelled or richly painted in vibrant colours to convey to the dazzled worshippers, who lived in pokey, smoke-filled hovels, something of the majesty of God and the wonders of Heaven which awaited repentant sinners. He stretched his imagination to the limit in order to find Christian symbolism in all the new architectural elements: he saw, for example, the ribs as representing the Prophets and Apostles, who were the carriers and upholders of Christianity.

Ribs had long been used as a purely decorative element in earlier buildings and the earliest known use of rib vaults occurs in Durham Cathedral (1093). Suger, however, was the first to build entirely in the new style. Between 1137 and 1144, he reconstructed parts of his abbey, and his example inspired the building of other Gothic churches in the Ile de France. Soon the style spread to other areas of France and beyond her borders.

Gothic architecture was born in the Abbey of St Denis, but many monastic foundations already had churches adequate for their needs. Most of the new-style Gothic cathedrals were built to serve the needs, not of monks, but the motley populations of the rapidly developing towns.

A misericord from Ripon Cathedral. c. 1494. Photo: Mercia MacDermott. Reproduced by kind permission of the Chapter.

Mediaeval society

The majority of the Green Men found in Gothic churches are different in style from those of the Renaissance period which we have just explored. They are also unlike those of the earlier Romanesque period which we have yet to visit in our search for the origin of the motif. In each era the outlook and priorities of the dominant classes played a part in determining the form of minor decorative elements, as well as whole buildings.

To have any chance of understanding what meaning the Green Men in Gothic churches may have had, we need to know something about the people who built these churches and worshipped in them. Indeed, the more we know the better but there is room in this book only for some basic information and a few signposts. Serious explorers will need to go further under their own steam!

Gothic architecture developed at a time when towns were beginning to assume greater economic and political importance. The long-established concept of Christian society as a three-fold entity, consisting of those who prayed (monks and clergy), those who fought (knights) and those who laboured (peasants), was being dented and called into question by the appearance of a new urban class of merchants and craftsmen. Tightly organized in guilds and confraternities, and proudly jealous of their liberties as townsfolk, the newcomers derived their status from wealth, rather than from birth or sanctity, and challenged the supremacy of feudal lords and clerics.

Then, as now, the world of commerce was a risky place and fortunes could be lost as well as won. Indeed, images of the Wheel of

*A foliate head in the choirstalls of Christ Church Cathedral, Oxford.
Photo: Mercia MacDermott. Reproduced by kind permission of the
Dean and Chapter of Christ Church Cathedral, Oxford.*

Fortune, borrowed from antiquity, appear in mediaeval art and churches. Naturally those with the greatest wealth played the leading role in civic affairs, including the building of cathedrals, but the very rich represented only a small percentage of those who crowded into the limited space within the walls which every city considered necessary to its safety and prestige. Princes, patricians, artisans, apprentices, vendors of this and that, bakers, vintners, labourers, beggars, prostitutes, musicians, clergy, friars, lawyers, physicians, foreigners, servants, thieves and philosophers all found a place in the urban communities for whom the great Gothic cathedrals were built.

In many cases almost everybody contributed something towards the construction of a cathedral or church, whose size and magnificence would reflect the community's pride in its city and itself. Not only kings, bishops and abbots, but also city councils, guilds and groups of citizens acted as initiators and patrons of ambitious building projects. Gothic cathedrals were so expensive and took so long to complete that often a succession of patrons and architects was involved in their construction.

Wealth in the form of money, rather than land, was suspect in the eyes of the Church. In the pre-Gothic churches, built mainly by monks, lurid carvings warned worshippers against *Avaritia* (greed for money) and its attendant vice, *Luxuria* (which may be translated as 'debauchery'). The mediaeval Church was particularly opposed to usury, and taught that eternal damnation awaited the money-lender, who lived without working by the sweat of his brow and earned interest even when he was asleep! Initially the Church made little distinction between moneylending, pure and simple, from which only the lender gained financially, and investment in commercial enterprises from which, if successful, all parties eventually profited. Even when the Church acknowledged the necessity for trade, it did not altogether cease to regard commerce as something shameful and degrading, and to condemn usury out of hand.

Among the most vehement critics of usury were the mendicant friars of the Dominican and Franciscan Orders, who, unlike most monks, were based in the towns and cities. They used stories known as *exempla* to illustrate the points made in their sermons. One of these concerned a freak accident, said to have occurred in Dijon in 1240, when a stone purse forming part of the figure of a condemned usurer in the carving of the Last Judgement above the church portal miraculously detached itself and fatally struck the head of a living usurer, who was attending a wedding! [Le Goff 1997: 250]

The merchants, for their part, were clearly worried, even fearful, about their fate in the next world, and there were many cases of rich men giving their wealth to the poor, late in life or in their wills. Merchants often meticulously recorded sums set aside for charity in their business accounts, in the hope that this would stand them in good stead on the Day of Judgement, since the greater the profit, the greater the donation. One successful merchant, Uomobuono Tucingo of Cremona (whose apt baptismal name means 'Good Man'), was so regular in his attendance at church and so generous in his charitable works that, when he died suddenly at Mass in 1197, Pope Innocent III yielded to clamour from his fellow-citizens and canonized him as St Homobonus a mere two years later!

Though guilty fears about the spiritual consequences of making money through trade persisted, they did not, of course, inhibit the growth of commerce. Some churchmen, like the Franciscan Berthold of Regensberg, sought theological formulae which would reconcile 'honest trading' with God's will and purpose. The development of the doctrine of Purgatory also provided some comfort for troubled consciences. This offered sinners a second chance to expiate their sins and avoid eternal damnation by spending an appropriate period of purification through torment in Purgatory. Here, as in the world of business, money appeared to talk. Those who could afford to do so left large sums for masses to be said for their souls preferably in specially built chantry chapels, in the belief that this would shorten their term in Purgatory and hasten their entry into Heaven.

The urge to save one's soul by renouncing personal wealth was a constant phenomenon during the Middle Ages. One expression of this urge was the foundation of orders of mendicant preaching friars, who relied on charity for support and who were approved by the Church. Another was the appearance of unofficial groups of lay people who attempted to follow the example of the Apostles and early Christians, who 'had all in common'. These groups included settled communities who, like the French *beghards* and *beguines*, lived semi-monastic lives without taking binding monastic vows, and a great assortment of itinerant preachers and would-be Messiahs [Cohn 1993; Lerner 1972].

Disaster and upheavals, such as war and epidemics, were common during the Middle Ages. Many people thought that these

A bench end in the parish church of St George, Bicknoller,
Somerset. 1534. The seed-capsules are poppy heads.
Photo: Ruth Wylie.

occurrences foretold the imminent appearance of the Antichrist and the start of the apocalyptic events which would lead to the establishment of a new heaven and a new earth, as described in the Book of Revelation (Chapters 20–21). Some felt that the Church itself was losing its way, and that the clergy, and even the Pope himself, had become too worldly and lacking in Christian virtues. As a result, there was always a ready audience for preachers who fuelled millenniarist hopes, identified the clergy with the Antichrist, proclaimed themselves to be the new Messiah, or offered new extreme ways of achieving salvation.

Many of these preachers, and even some harmless members of settled lay communities, were accused by the Church of heresy and all manner of immorality. The same allegations of shocking practices, couched in almost the same words and generally unsubstantiated, were regularly trotted out against groups and individuals as diverse as the Cathars, *beguines* and so-called 'Free Spirits'.

Throughout the Middle Ages, heresies, extremist movements and religious persecutions formed a constant undercurrent, and we need to be aware of them. So far absolutely no evidence has been found to support the speculation that some Green Men might reflect this undercurrent.

The changes in the siting and patronage of cathedrals affected certain aspects of architecture and decoration, apart from the main structural ones. Most cathedrals were now built within walled cities, amid a labyrinth of narrow streets and jumbled houses, where space was at a premium. An uninterrupted view of the building was often possible only from one direction, and therefore the main external decoration was concentrated on that side of the cathedral. In most cases, this was the west front, where the main portals opened onto an approach road or town square. West fronts were often adorned with serried ranks of the great and good: Apostles, Old Testament Patriarchs, saints and kings and queens.

Scenes of the Last Judgement and depictions of the Vices were fewer, less prominent and less horrific than in monastic churches. Unlike the monks, who had renounced the world and its vanities, the townsfolk (especially the more affluent and influential) were firmly rooted in material things, and preferred to dwell on the rewards of virtue rather than the punishment of sin. The new cathedrals, filled with colour and light, were designed to give the worshipper a foretaste of Paradise, and so the decoration placed the emphasis on the joys of Heaven, rather than the horrors of Hell.

A double-headed roof-boss in the cloisters of the Cathedral of the Holy Trinity, Norwich, Norfolk. Fourteenth to fifteenth century. Photo: Ruth Wylie. Reproduced by kind permission of the Chapter of Norwich Cathedral.

While grandiose west fronts offered patrons and artisans opportunities to create sublime spectacles of holiness, other aspects of the new style of architecture provided suitable sites for small-scale artistic initiative. Prominent among them were the intersections of the ribs that supported the roofs of naves, aisles, chapels and cloisters. These could be enlivened with carved roof-bosses of a decorative or didactic nature. Like misericords, arm-rests, and other parts of choir-stalls, roof-bosses soon became a favourite haunt of foliate heads.

*Multiple Green Men on a roof-boss in the church of St Mary,
Haverfordwest, Pembrokeshire. Early sixteenth century.
Photo: Ruth Wylie.*

Before examining the Green Men associated with Gothic architecture, we shall take a brief look at the gardens of the period. By so doing we shall gain further insight into the intriguing workings of the mediaeval mind and may find some clue to the meaning of the Gothic Green Man.

Mediaeval gardens and attitudes towards nature

The early years of Gothic architecture coincided with the reappearance of gardens purely for pleasure. Such gardens had existed in Roman times and still existed in countries under Islamic rule. For many centuries after the collapse of the Roman Empire, however, the only gardens in western Europe were those where plants were grown either for food or for medicinal purposes, as they were in monasteries. Charlemagne (742–814) encouraged the revival of garden-making, but it was from the thirteenth century, onwards that gardens really become popular, both in art and literature and in reality.

Mediaeval people loved flowers and trees, but they made no attempt to identify with nature. On the contrary, they tried to tame it for their own enjoyment in small, manageable, well-fenced units. The wildwood was too wild and too dangerous, and the forest was the province of those rich enough to exploit its resources by hunting or for timber. The mediaeval garden, or herber, was essentially a tiny Garden of Eden: an enclosed space, usually under an acre in size, protected against the outside world. Inside, there would be grassy banks to sit upon, herbaceous borders, trellises, a bower or a shady alley of pleached trees (trees closely planted in two rows and carefully trained and pruned so that their intertwined branches form a continuous tunnel), a lawn – either green and close cut, or studded with daisies, with a fountain in the middle, and, perhaps, a small 'flowery mead'. Richer people with more space might also have an enclosed orchard, and even a much larger, but also enclosed, pleasure garden, where wild animals were kept to be looked at and not hunted.

Small private herbers appeared in the growing towns and cities, where people first began to feel the need to have some contact with nature, albeit of a severely domesticated kind. Such gardens were the prerogative of the upper classes. The ladies would sit at leisure in a fragrant green oasis, well insulated against the outside world, and, indeed, against Nature in her freer, more natural form.

Mediaeval Christians endowed everything possible with religious symbolism, and they made the herber, or *hortus conclusus* (enclosed garden) a metaphor for the Virgin Mary, whose cult was becoming increasingly popular. The idea of the *hortus conclusus* originated in those verses of the Song of Solomon – written in a very different context – which state: 'A garden enclosed is my sister, my spouse; a spring shut up, a fountain sealed. Thy plants are an orchard of pomegranates, with pleasant fruits; camphire, with spikenard, spikenard and saffron; calamus and cinnamon, with all trees of frankincense; myrrh and aloes, with all the chief spices; a fountain of gardens, a well of living water, and streams from Lebanon.' (Song of Solomon, 4.12–15). Much of our knowledge of the appearance of mediaeval gardens and the flowers grown in them is derived from

A roof-boss in the gatehouse of Jumièges Abbey, Seine Maritime, Normandy. Thirteenth century. Photo: Ruth Wylie.

paintings of 'Mary Gardens', i.e. pictures of the Virgin sitting in just such an enclosed garden, in which the plants are not only recognizable, but also had symbolic Christian meanings.

The leaves of Southwell

During the thirteenth century, when enclosed gardens and plant symbolism were popular, naturalistic leaves began to replace stiff, stylized foliage in a number of newly-built cathedrals. Some thirty different species of plants and flowers have been identified in Reims Cathedral, and the new fashion was copied in several other cathedrals, including Naumburg, Magdeburg, Leon, Chartres, and Lincoln.

Lincoln Cathedral has an unusual Green Man at the base of an arch of naturalistic foliage which leads into the choir aisle. For Green Man enthusiasts, however, the best place to see the motif combined with botanically accurate stone plants is Southwell Minster, Nottinghamshire.

Southwell Minster was founded in Anglo-Saxon times, and a fragment of Anglo-Saxon carving, including a wyvern with a coiling, leafy appendage, is preserved over a door in the west wall of the Romanesque north transept, The Minster was a collegiate foundation within the Diocese of York. It was governed by a Chapter of secular canons, who had not taken monastic vows but were priests in Holy Orders in receipt of a prebend, or special stipend.

About the middle of the twelfth century the original Anglo-Saxon church had been replaced by a Romanesque one whose nave, transepts and towers (crossing and western) are still standing. During the first half of the thirteenth century the Chapter decided to demolish the Romanesque chancel and build a much larger choir (or quire) in the new Gothic style. Towards the end of the thirteenth century, they added a glorious octagonal Chapter House with huge windows and carved foliage remarkable both for its profusion and its naturalistic precision.

The Chapter House is entered from the north side of the choir through a passage where all the archways and capitals are decorated as though for a festival, with garlands and bunches of exquisitely carved vegetation. Around the walls of the Chapter House there are thirty-six seats, separated by columns with leafy capitals. Above each seat is a trefoil arch, surmounted by a leafy gable, and in each case the tympanum (the space between the arch and the gable) is richly decorated.

In six of the thirty-six tympana there are heads disgorging various types of foliage, mainly plants rather than trees. In the seventh a pensive young man, with a foliage-spewing Green Man as his neighbour, gazes out intently from behind sprays of hawthorn, which he holds apart with his hands. There is also a hawthorn mask, with leaves arising from its chin and forehead, above the abacus of a capital decorated with flowering hawthorn. The ninth foliate head in the Chapter House is on a corbel and disgorges ivy to the right and maple to the left. One tympanum in the Chapter House contains an example of foliate tails: two reptiles, whose linked tails turn into sprigs of hawthorn with berries.

In two of the tympana containing Green Men, birds are also present. In one, they peck at sprouting buttercups and, in the other,

at an ivy stem and a smaller bird, possibly a chick. Birds in combination with Green Men are fairly rare. Other examples occur in the Chapter House of Noyon Cathedral (Oise, France), where they are seen stealing grapes from a vine disgorged by a pleasant-faced Green Man, and at Sutton Benger (Wiltshire), where finely sculpted birds, reminiscent of William Morris's 'Strawberry Thieves', are eating berries from a mass of hawthorn emerging from the mouth of one of the most celebrated Green Men. This Green Man has an unusually intelligent and refined face, and, although he is believed to date from the thirteenth or fourteenth century, some re-working may have been done by Victorian restorers.

In 1933, Professor A.C. Seward made a systematic study of the leaves of Southwell, with a view to identifying them botanically. Not

Opposite: *A face peeps through fruiting hawthorn branches in one
of the tympana of the Chapter House of the Minster of the Blessed
Virgin Mary, Southwell, Nottinghamshire. c.1290.*

Above: *A head disgorging ivy, with two birds and a fledgeling, in a
tympanum in the Chapter House of the Minster of the Blessed Virgin
Mary, Southwell, Nottinghamshire. c.1290.*

Photos: *Ruth Wylie. Reproduced by kind permission of the Dean
and Chapter of Southwell.*

85

*One of the many Green Men in the tympana of the Chapter House
of the Minster of the Blessed Virgin Mary, Southwell,
Nottinghamshire. c.1290. The plants have been identified as
buttercups and hops. Photo: Ruth Wylie. Reproduced by kind
permission of the Dean and Chapter of Southwell.*

all could be identified beyond doubt, but he was able to establish
that maple leaves were the favourite choice, occurring some thirty
times in the one hundred and forty examples examined. Oak came
next, with twenty-six examples, followed by hawthorn (nineteen or
twenty examples), ranunculus (buttercups) and potentilla (nineteen),

and vine (eighteen). Together, these account for over eighty percent of the examples, with ivy, hops, and two examples each of rose and bryony as part of the remaining twenty percent [Seward 1933–34: 1–32].

The leaves appear to have been chosen for their decorative qualities rather than for their magical significance. The maple so favoured by the Southwell masons does not figure prominently in English folklore as a magic tree. Neither, strangely, does the oak, although it is universally venerated for its size, long life and strength, and often served as a boundary marker, or place of assembly. Hawthorn is, indeed, a magical plant associated with a whole range of rites and superstitions, but these are almost all centred on the flowers, (i.e. the May blossom) while, as often as not, it is the fruit which the Southwell and other masons chose to depict in addition to the leaves. For obvious reasons buttercups were included in May Day garlands and rituals aimed at increasing the quality of dairy produce, while potentilla was believed to protect against witches and to cure fevers. Potentilla's alternative name of Cinquefoil gives the clue to its popularity with masons, since its five-fingered leaf is exceedingly decorative, like those of the maple, oak and buttercup.

The leaves themselves are the most important element in Southwell, and the Green Men seem subordinate to the wonderful foliage in the same way that vases are subordinate to the flowers which they display. The actual heads are not particularly striking, and their expressions tend to be calm and untroubled. The same can also be said of the foliate figures on the Minster's unusual fourteenth-century misericords. On one, a man in a long robe sits in a relaxed position, with his hands resting on his knees, calmly disgorging huge leaves to left and right. On another, two jolly twins embrace each other, with foliage, flowers and grapes emerging like tails from under their short tunics. On a third, a curious figure, with a human head and a body reminiscent of a grub or woodlouse, contentedly strokes foliage arising from a tail, which it holds in front of itself with its other hand. More foliage flows behind it from the tip of its cap.

Green Man enthusiasts tend to notice Green Men to the exclusion of all else, and explorers bent on assessing the significance of the Green Men of Southwell need to bear in mind that they represent only a small part of the decoration as a whole. Many other images appear among the famous greenery. On one capital, for example, two boars eat acorns among huge oak-leaves; on another, a hare is cornered by two hounds among ivy. There are also numerous other motifs, including heads, both portraits and caricatures, dragon-

A thirteenth-century misericord in the Minster of the Blessed Virgin Mary, Southwell, Nottinghamshire. Photo: Ruth Wylie. Reproduced by kind permission of the Dean and Chapter of Southwell.

like creatures, lions, a ram, a dog, a bull, a merman, a man gathering grapes, a goatherd and goat, and sundry birds.

Elsewhere, Green Men also occur among naturalistically carved foliage, but not in such great numbers as to make them part and parcel of the style. In Reims Cathedral, for example, the inner west wall is decorated with fifty-two niches containing Old Testament figures, framed by panels and spandrels filled with naturalistically carved leaves and flowers. There are, however, only two Green Men – both of them stereotype leaf-masks which occur in the spandrels on either side of just one of the fifty-two niches.

The naturalistic style did not catch on everywhere, neither did it last. By the fifteenth century, there was a return to more abstract forms of foliage.

Green Men with recognizable foliage occur not only in those cathedrals noted for their naturalistically carved vegetation. They can also be found in other, less leafy, sites. The most popular foliage includes oak, ivy and vines. The Green Man roof-bosses of Exeter Cathedral are unusual in disgorging what may be either wormwood (*Artemisia absinthium*), or mugwort (*Artemisia vulgaris*), or possibly even silverweed (*Potentilla anserina*). The vast majority of Gothic Green Men, however, have vegetation to which one could not hazard a name.

Where to look and what to look for

Examples of foliate heads can be found in virtually every Gothic cathedral, and in many parish churches as well. Part of the pleasure of visiting them lies in searching for Green Men and coming upon them unawares. But beware! Always make sure that you look properly, and, if possible, do some homework or take advice before you go. There is nothing more galling for a Green Man enthusiast than to visit a wonderful church, only to discover, when it is too late, that you have missed something important!

Some cathedrals built in the new Gothic style during the thirteenth century already contain several types of Green Man, including both leaf-masks and heads sprouting or spewing out vegetation. These proliferated in an astonishing range of imaginative variations throughout the fourteenth and fifteenth centuries. Capitals, corbels, doorways, porches, canopied tombs, fonts, roof-bosses, choir-stalls, misericords, Lady Chapels, and Easter Sepulchres are among the more promising sites. Some churches are so rich in foliate figures that even the most assiduous spotter may fail to notice a few less obvious examples.

Italianate heads are, of course, absent, and, if the building is pure Gothic, so are the characteristic Romanesque 'cat-faces' which, for some unknown reason, became extinct following the introduction of pointed arches. Such is the profusion of new images that their absence is not missed.

There is nothing grotesque, menacing or anguished about the early Gothic heads of Southwell, but this is by no means the norm. Many Gothic Green Men look haggard, wrathful, malevolent, aggressive, or despairing. Some leer or snarl, or stick out their tongues. Some are plainly demons, while others seem to be suffocating in their foliage, or being consumed by it.

The least variable of foliate heads is the perennial leaf-mask, because the concept itself imposes certain limitations. The leaves used to create such faces are usually non-botanical, or stylized acanthus, with the nose, eyes and lips taking the simplest of human forms. Despite these limitations, this genre has provided what is possibly the most striking and unforgettable Green Man ever created. This is the mask composed of a single acanthus leaf on the plinth supporting the statue of the Rider in Bamberg Cathedral (c.1237). Exceptionally, it is oblong in shape, unlike the majority of leaf-masks, which tend to be rhomboid, roughly triangular, or five-pointed like a vine or maple-leaf.

A face or simply foliage? The Cathedral porch, Villefranche-de-Rouergue, Aveyron, France. Photo: Mercia MacDermott.

A few foliate designs are composed entirely of leaves arranged in such a way that they suggest a face without actually having any human features. Unlike other leaf-masks, which have added eyes, noses, lips, etc., these rely on such devices as curls in a leaf and hollowed-out spaces between the leaves to produce the effect of a face. In some cases, the 'face' is plain to see, while in others it may exist only in the imagination of eager Green Man spotters.

In comparison with leaf-masks, the 'spewers' and 'sprouters' are far more varied, both botanically and in composition. In the most common form, the vegetation proceeds from the mouth in twin shoots which curl upwards, outwards, or downwards. In many cases, leaves may emerge – instead of or in addition to the mouth – from the nostrils, the corners of the eyes, the eyebrows, the upper lips (like moustaches), the cheeks, the temples, the centre of the forehead, the top of the head, and, more rarely, the ears. Occasionally - and these are, perhaps, the most unpleasant and disturbing images of all - the leaves sprout from the eye-sockets like some parasitic growth that has blotted out the light. These are totally different in character and effect to the Renaissance image on the picture frame described in the previous chapter.

Most Gothic Green Men are, to a greater or lesser extent, distorted or grotesque in appearance. Some are cross-eyed. Some have irregular or unpleasantly prominent teeth. Many have their tongues out, and a few even have double tongues. Some have beards, either leafy or hairy. Some have horns, and some have ears more like those of animals than humans. Most are bareheaded, while a few have leaves in place of hair, and some have crowns or various other types of headgear. A few even appear to have employed skilled hairdressers!

Occasionally Green Men occur in pairs, as on a roof-boss in Exeter Cathedral, or in clusters – a fine example can be found on a boss in the south aisle of Chichester Cathedral (see photo on next page), where a ring of six interlocking faces share six eyes between them. In Chartres Cathedral, near Paris, there is a group of three thirteenth-century heads, side by side above the portal of the south transept. The central head is an acanthus leaf-mask, while its companions to either side respectively disgorge vines with grapes and oak-leaves with acorns.

Some Green Men have triple faces – one full and two in profile, with the latter disgorging foliage. Triple heads representing certain local deities occur in the art of Celtic tribes, both in the Gallo-Roman

Six Green Men with just six eyes between them. A roof-boss in the south choir aisle of the Cathedral of the Holy Trinity, Chichester, West Sussex. Early thirteenth century. Photo: Ruth Wylie.

period and earlier. They were particularly associated with the Remi – a tribe who lived in northeastern Gaul around present-day Reims, but examples have also been found in other areas, including Provence, the Dordogne, Scotland and Ireland [Green 1994: 171–9]. These Celtic heads could have provided the inspiration for the later mediaeval ones, but, unlike the latter, they were never foliate and never disgorged leaves. Triplication was common in Celtic art, both in the form of heads alone, and in the form of separate identical figures. Its probable purpose was to emphasize and augment the power of the image by repetition. In mediaeval Christian art, triple heads, or 'tricephaloi', can convey two entirely contradictory meanings: they can represent either the Holy Trinity or Triceps Beelzebub, Prince of Hell! This makes things difficult for Green Man explorers, and each example requires individual interpretation.

A face or not a face? A misericord from a Benedictine monastery in Ghent, Belgium, now in the church of St Andrew, Gatton, Surrey. c.1500. This misericord is one of several in the same style. All the others have clearly defined faces with various expressions.
Photo: Ruth Wylie.

There seems little doubt as to the infernal nature of the impressive tricephaloi on the facade of the twelfth-century church of San Pietro in Tuscania (Viterbo, Italy). These are situated above and below an unglazed window with three columns. The lower tricephalos has a torso and arms, with which he embraces a large serpent. From his two mouths in profile there emerge stems which coil upwards, enclosing leafy medallions, a dragon, and two half-human, half-monster figures. These stems enter the side mouths of the upper figure, which consists simply of a triple head with two horns. The tongues of both central faces are protruding, and recognizable among the vegetation are two large poppy seed-heads, close to the side mouths of the lower tricephalos. As the source of opium, poppy seed-heads generally symbolize sleep or death. This particular composition is, as far as I know, unique.

The same infernal association can probably be assigned to the disgorging tricephaloi found on rare English fifteenth-century

A wooden roof-boss in the church of St Mary, Chagford, Devon.
Photo: Ruth Wylie.

misericords. Misericords were usually sites for grotesque and humorously profane carvings. It seems unlikely that the monks of Whalley Abbey (Lancashire) or Cartmel Priory (Cumbria), for whom the tricephalic misericords were made, would have been so blasphemous as to rest their backsides on the Holy Trinity!

On the other hand, you can never tell! What shocks us would not necessarily have shocked mediaeval people, and vice versa. Who knows for certain whether the monks, seated upon their tricephalic misericords, saw themselves as subduing Beelzebub or as supported in their infirmity by the Holy Trinity?

In St Mary and All Saints in Whalley (once the church of a Cistercian Abbey), the carvings on the misericords include a wife hitting her husband with a frying-pan, a single-faced, bearded head

*A nave roof-boss in the Priory Church of SS Mary and Cuthbert at
Bolton Abbey, North Yorkshire. Sixteenth century.
Photo: Ruth Wylie.*

disgorging foliage, and a tricephalos with two other heads in profile
as supporters, dangling on stems which emerge from its side mouths.
Little remains of Cartmel Priory apart from the gatehouse and the
church, where, on one of the misericords, there is a fine tricephalos,
with a crown, a wrinkled brow and corkscrew-curled moustaches
and beard (see photograph page 98).

As we have already seen in Southwell Minster, not all foliate
heads fall into one of the two main categories of leaf-masks and
disgorgers. Some merely peep out through foliage which surrounds
them but does not form part of them. In most cases, the foliage fits
quite closely around the face, especially if the motif occurs on a roof-
boss. Examples of 'peerers' can be seen on the tomb of St Frideswide

in Oxford Cathedral; on a section of a screen made for Siena Cathedral in the third quarter of the thirteenth-century (now in the Victoria and Albert Museum), and in the vestibule of York Minster's Chapter House.

Occasionally faces are surrounded with leaves or petals so that they resemble anthropomorphic flowers. Leaf-ringed faces can be found in company with spewing Green Men and various animal and tongue-showing masks on the roof-bosses in the cloisters of Canterbury Cathedral. 'Flower-faces' are especially numerous in Gloucester Cathedral, where they appear on bosses in the north aisle of the nave and in the south porch. Unlike most other foliate heads, 'flower-faces' are generally smiling, like representations of the Sun.

Most Green Men are simply severed heads but a few have limbs and bodies. Apart from those already mentioned in the section about Southwell Minster other notable examples can be seen in the spandrels of the early fourteenth-century choir-stalls of Winchester Cathedral. Here, in addition to profile heads disgorging tangles of leafy branches, there are also complete figures, clothed like mediaeval warriors in tunics and armed with swords and bucklers, with sprays of foliage sprouting from their mouths.

Sometimes the roles of man and leaf are reversed, so that heads grow out of foliage instead of emitting it, Yet another variation on the half-plant, half-human theme is the design in which the head and torso of a man or woman rises like a flower-spike or fruit from a basis of vegetation. Good examples can be seen on the tympanum of the Royal Portal of Chartres Cathedral in France.

Some Green Men do not have flesh at all, but are merely skulls, placed in *memento mori* situations, as in Haddon Hall chapel, in Derbyshire (fourteenth to fifteenth centuries).

We have yet to explore the typically Romanesque 'cat-faces' which disgorge long stems rather than leaves. Although these went out of fashion with round arches, foliate animals of a different design continued to be popular in the Gothic period and were treated in the same style as human heads. Often, on closer examination, a particularly repulsive foliate head on a boss or poppy-head bench-end will turn out to be a lion – the beast most favoured by carvers. Other animals, however, do occur, and one fine example – a dog-like creature disgorging greenery – can be seen, unusually situated, at the *base* of one of the pillars in the Trinity Chapel in Salisbury Cathedral.

Explorers wishing to find and compare a great variety of Green Men in the form of bosses should visit the cloisters of Norwich

*A double-headed roof-boss in the retro-choir of the Cathedral of
St Peter, Exeter, Devon. Early fourteenth century. The foliage is
mugwort or wormwood. Photo: Ruth Wylie. Reproduced by kind
permission of the Dean and Chapter of Exeter.*

Cathedral, rebuilt in the fourteenth century after the original
Romanesque ones were destroyed in a riot in 1272. Here, among
some four hundred bosses depicting everything from scenes from the
Book of Revelation and the lives of the saints to a windmill and an
owl, there are clusters of leaves – oak, hawthorn, grapes and wild
rose – and at least a dozen or more wonderful foliate heads.

The cloisters of Canterbury Cathedral (early fifteenth century) are
also rich in foliate heads of various kinds. Unusually, some of those
who are shown peeping through leaves rather than disgorging them
actually appear to be laughing.

For sheer numbers of Green Men within a relatively small area,
the ancient buildings of Oxford are hard to beat. Numerous heads
can be found in college chapels (e.g. New College), cloisters and

A tricephalos misericord in the priory church of SS Mary and Michael, Cartmel, Cumbria. 1416–41. Photo: Ruth Wylie.

passage ways (e.g. Magdalen), and entrances and exteriors (e.g. Pembroke, Magdalen, and Merton). Not all of them, of course, are mediaeval. Some are eighteenth or nineteenth-century restorations or additions. Many are Renaissance. One, at least, in the garden of St Edmund Hall, is late twentieth century (see page 189).

Green Man explorers will sometimes find visits to small country churches as rewarding as those to great cathedrals. Interesting examples, often carved in wood rather than stone, can be found as roof-bosses (fourteenth or fifteenth century) in churches in Devon, such as St Andrew's in South Tawton and St Andrew's in Sampford Courtenay. Many of these are neither happy not serene, but look hostile, tormented or even close to death, with bared teeth or protruding tongues. Some of the more afflicted and moribund may reflect the terror of the Black Death, which decimated whole populations on the Continent and in England during the middle of the fourteenth century.

One remote parish church – Hawton in Nottinghamshire – has a rare example of a Green Man with protruding tongue and foliage growing out of its ears carved on the spandrel of an Easter Sepulchre (see photograph on page 100). Few Easter Sepulchres have survived in England, and many people are no longer aware of their existence and role in the symbolic re-enactment of Christ's burial and resurrection which, prior to the Reformation, began on Maundy Thursday and continued until Easter morning.

Easter Sepulchres were often moveable structures, consisting of a wooden frame covered with rich cloths, brought into the church when required and then removed again after standing empty from

One of the several 'flower-faces' in the Cathedral of St Peter and the Holy Trinity, Gloucester. This roof-boss in the south porch is nineteenth century. A similar one can be seen in the north aisle.
Photo: Ruth Wylie.

Easter Day until the Friday after Easter. In some churches, however, they consisted of a special recess built into the wall on the north side of the chancel (as is the case at Hawton), or a chamber built into the tomb of a parishioner sufficiently pious and wealthy to leave money for the purpose. Lincoln Cathedral has a richly carved thirteenth-century Easter Sepulchre, and examples can still be found in a few parish churches, including Heckington, Navenby and Irnham (all in Lincolnshire). Hawton's Easter Sepulchre is the most elaborate to survive in a parish church.

On the Continent, chapels containing sculpted figures representing the Entombment or the Lamentation over the dead Christ are widespread. Unlike the English Easter Sepulchre, these chapels were not used for any special rites in connection with Easter, but simply for contemplation and meditation on stories connected with the Crucifixion and Mary's experiences and sufferings. This type of chapel is also sometimes decorated with foliate heads, as is the

*Foliate head on the Easter Sepulchre, All Saints church, Hawton,
Nottinghamshire. Photo: Mercia MacDermott.*

case in the Minster in Freiburg im Breisgau, Germany (c.1330),
where the columns of the sepulchre containing a sculpture of the
dead Christ, watched over by mourning figures, are decorated with
heads disgorging greenery. The same Minster has a spectacular
openwork octagonal spire, each of whose eight ribs, decorated with
leafy stems, rises from a head.

During the Gothic period, personal tombs and memorials were
sometimes decorated with Green Men, though less frequently than in
post-Renaissance times. The shrine of St Frideswide (c.1289) in
Oxford Cathedral, for example, is decorated with several heads of
serene appearance, peering through leaves which are naturalistically
carved and have been identified as maple, hawthorn, greater
celandine, bryony, sycamore, oak, vine and ivy [Rice-Oxley.1934:
212], (see photo page 103).

A Green Man, with large stylized leaves emerging from his
nostrils and smaller leaves instead of hair, can be seen at the foot of
the recumbent effigy of William Harrington, who was rector of St
Chad's, Harpswell, in Lincolnshire, and died in 1350. Harrington's
more illustrious contemporary, Robert Stratford, who was Bishop of
Chichester from 1337–62, also has a Green Man at his feet, but
situated above them on the ceiling of his canopy tomb in the south
transept of Chichester Cathedral. This Green Man is disgorging
stylized foliage from its mouth.

*A foliate animal at the base of a pillar in the Trinity Chapel
of the Cathedral of the Blessed Virgin Mary, Salisbury.
Photo: Mercia MacDermott.*

The enormous variety of Gothic foliate images obliges us
seriously to consider the possibility that mediaeval Christians did not
necessarily regard all these forms as being aspects of one and the
same image, and that the differences in design may indicate
differences in symbolism and purpose.

There is no uniformity of design even when Green Men are used
for a similar purpose, such as to adorn a tomb. Do leaves emerging
from the mouth convey a different message to those emerging from
the nose? What are the 'peepers' on St Frideswide's shrine trying to
tell us? Are those in Southwell's Chapter House saying the same
thing?

There are no easy answers to these questions, but in the next
section we shall follow up a few possible clues by looking at
mediaeval literature.

What we can learn from mediaeval best-sellers

In mediaeval times few people could read. Indeed, prior to the
invention of printing, books were a luxury that few could afford. Most
of the laboriously hand-copied books of the period were
commissioned and owned by kings, nobles and religious
foundations. In Western Europe the use of Latin, rather than the
vernacular, further limited public access to literature.

During the twelfth and thirteenth centuries the first universities were founded, closely linked to the Church and concentrating on the study of subjects related to theology and Christian morality. The rising class of merchants and mastercraftsmen could manage without instruction in such matters, but they needed to be able to keep accurate accounts, to write legible business letters, and even to have some understanding of foreign languages if they traded with other countries. This need led to the development in towns and cities of lay schools, both private and municipal, offering the necessary tuition.

For the illiterate majority, however, the spoken word of the clergy, monks and friars, illustrated by the carvings, frescoes and pictorial windows in the local church or cathedral, took the place of books. Many of these images were copied by craftsmen from illuminated manuscripts made available to them by clients. Some masons had specialized sketchbooks in which they recorded new ideas picked up on their travels and sample designs to offer their clients. The only mediaeval book of this kind known to have survived is the sketchbook compiled by Villard de Honnecourt in the late 1220s. Its contents include illustrations of tools and building practices, hints on applied geometry, drawing of elevations and rose windows, and designs for sculpted figures, both human and animal, taken from bestiaries, ivories, and other sources. Among these designs are the leaf-masks referred to in Chapter 1.

For centuries during the Middle Ages, the books known as bestiaries enjoyed enduring popularity among both those who could read and those to whom their subject matter was conveyed by word of mouth. Bestiaries consisted of illustrations and engaging descriptions – some fact, much fiction and fantasy – of various animals, whose habits, real or imagined, were given a symbolic or didactic Christian meaning. Often these meanings were ambivalent or contradictory. A donkey, for example, could be viewed either as a model of patience and humility, or as the incarnation of stupidity and obstinacy. Lions could be seen as voracious adversaries or noble guardians, and even as a symbol of Christ himself.

Bestiaries were ultimately derived from a Greek work entitled *Physiologus* (The Naturalist) and compiled by an unknown author about the fourth century AD, or earlier, probably in Alexandria. It was copied again and again, and translated into many languages, including Ethiopian, Syriac and Armenian. It first appeared in Latin during the eighth century. In the course of copying and translation, new information and more creatures were added to the original nucleus, so that twelfth and thirteenth-century bestiaries have double

The tomb of St Frideswide in the Lady Chapel of Christ Church Cathedral, Oxford. 1289. Photo: Ruth Wylie. By kind permission of the Dean and Chapter of Christ Church Cathedral, Oxford.

or treble the number of entries as the original *Physiologus*. Most of the creatures described are ordinary domestic and wild animals, but there is a fair sprinkling of monsters and mythical beasts, to which we will return in the next chapter. (English translations of mediaeval bestiaries, with illustrations, include T.S. White, *The Book of Beasts*. 1954, and Richard Barber, *Bestiary*. 1999.)

Bestiaries are the key to many of the weird and wonderful carvings found in churches. Mediaeval worshippers were familiar with the tales and symbolic meanings attached to each creature, and

103

would have been suitably edified when they saw them reproduced in stone and wood. Although unicorns, dragons, mermaids, and various plants and trees are among the fabulous and mundane items described in bestiaries, there are no Green Men, or anything remotely suggestive of them. This omission could, in itself, be significant, and is worth pondering over.

Another popular mediaeval book, which may indeed have some bearing on the presence of Green Men in churches, is the work known in England as *The Golden Legend* and written by Jacobus de Voragine (or Voraigne) between 1255 and 1266. Jacobus was born about 1228 or 1230 at Varaggio, or Varazze, on the Gulf of Genoa. He entered the Dominican Order in 1244, and eventually became Archbishop of Genoa in 1292. On his death in 1298 he was venerated as a saint, and in 1816 he was officially beatified.

Jacobus called his book *Legenda Sanctorum* (Legends of the Saints), and, indeed, it consists mainly of attractively edifying stories about the saints, the miracles which they wrought, and their heroic struggles against the Devil and other adversaries. He collected his material from all kinds of sources, including earlier hagiographical literature and folk tales, and the book was designed to inspire believers and to strengthen their faith and resolve. Christian example, rather than historical truth, was Jacobus's aim, and he would sometimes include more than one version of an event and, on occasions, even admit that he was not sure of the veracity of something which, nevertheless, made a good moral story!

The Golden Legend is divided into four parts, corresponding to the Church's year. In addition to the lives of the saints it contains information about the life and mission of Christ, likewise culled from many sources, including apocryphal books not admitted to the Vulgate or Authorized Version of the Bible. The chapter entitled *The Finding of the True Cross* is of most interest to Green Man explorers because it contains a long and complicated story of how part of the wood used to construct the Cross came from a shoot of a tree which Adam's son, Seth, obtained from the Archangel Michael and planted on his father's grave.

The shoot grew to be a great tree, which was admired by Solomon, but could not be used in the construction of one of his houses (I Kings, 7) because it did not seem to fit anywhere. Instead it was made into a bridge. When the visiting Queen of Sheba intuitively realized that the Saviour of the World would one day hang upon that very wood and that, through His death, the kingdom of the Jews would be destroyed, Solomon had the wood taken out and buried deep in the earth. Later, a pond, identified with the Pool of Bethesda (John 5.2–4), welled up on the spot. Just before the Crucifixion, the piece of wood floated up to the surface and was used by the Jews to make the Cross. After a period of being hidden in the ground, the True Cross was rediscovered by Helena, whose son, the Byzantine Emperor Constantine, made Christianity the official religion of his Empire, having dreamt of the Cross on the eve of a decisive battle. [Jacobus de Voragine, trans. William Granges Ryan 1993: 277–8]

In retelling this story, Jacobus made use of several sources which give slightly different versions of Seth's transactions with the Archangel. From the apocryphal *Gospel of Nicodemus* (Chapter 14) he took a version in which Adam, already ill and infirm, sent Seth to the Gates of Paradise to ask the Archangel for some oil from the Tree of Mercy, which, he believed, could restore his health and vigour. The Archangel Michael told Seth that there was no way in which he could obtain it until 5,500 years had gone by, that is until the coming of Christ. Chapters 19 and 20 of the *Gospel of Nicodemus* describe how eventually Adam greeted Jesus and was brought out of Hell into Heaven.

Jacobus also offers his readers two more anonymous versions in which Michael gives cuttings to Seth – an essential element in the long miraculous saga of the True Cross. In one, the Archangel gives Seth a shoot from the Tree of Mercy, and orders him to plant it on the Mount of Lebanon. In the other, the shoot comes from the very tree under which Adam committed his original sin, and Seth is told that when the shoot bears fruit, meaning when Jesus hangs from the Cross, his father will be made whole. Seth plants the shoot on Adam's grave and sets in motion the chain of events which eventually lead to its being used for the Crucifixion.

In addition to the versions included by Jacobus in *The Golden Legend*, other variants of what the Archangel is supposed to have given to Seth, and what the latter did with the gift, were also in circulation during the Middle Ages. Of particular interest to us is the variant on which Piero della Francesca (1410–20 to 1492) based his cycle of frescoes illustrating the Legend of the True Cross in the church of San Francesco in Arezzo (1459). Here, Adam asks Seth to obtain oil from the Tree of Mercy, but, instead, the Archangel gives him seeds from the Tree of Sin, and instructs him to place them in his father's *mouth* when he is dead. Seth arrives home to find him already dead, and duly places the seeds in his mouth, from whence they grow into the mighty tree felled by Solomon. In one of Piero's frescoes, a leafy sapling can be seen emerging from Adam's mouth.

Seeds, trees and sprouting vegetation occur in all these versions of a popular legend associated with the redemption of Adam and, therefore, of all Mankind. Even before such legends were current, Christians often viewed the Cross not as dead wood but as a tree. When, for example, the Emperor Theodosius I (379–95) decided to erect a golden cross in Jerusalem, he had it made in the form of a plant encrusted with jewels [Schama 1996: 214]. Crosses sprouting or adorned with leaves are common in mediaeval art. A crucifix with a foliate cross, dating from the twelfth century can just be seen, roughly carved into the rock, in the Hermit's Cave, near Robin Hood's Stride, in Derbyshire.

Such associations could account for at least some of the Green Man carvings in churches. It might explain why, for example, Green Men appear on fonts, such as the fourteenth-century one in the church of St Mary the Virgin in Leckhampstead, Buckinghamshire, where an oak tree, complete with a trunk, branches, leaves and acorns, emerges from the mouth of a smallish head.

The legendary link between Adam's sapling and the redeeming Cross could also explain why Green Men are sometimes found in close proximity to images of the Virgin Mary, mother of the Redeemer.

Examples of this can be seen in the choir of Exeter Cathedral on two corbels dating from the end of the thirteenth or beginning of the fourteenth century. One corbel shows the Virgin holding the Child and standing on the head of a Green Man, with a flying angel above her – all surrounded by the gilded leaves which the Green Man disgorges. The second corbel shows the Coronation of the Virgin above an angel playing a viol on the head of a Green Man, whose leaves frame the whole scene.

In the nave of the same Cathedral, there is another corbel depicting the Coronation of the Virgin, above an image of the Virgin and Child, supported not by a Green Man this time, but by Jesse, out of whose loins the framing vegetation grows. Jesse was the father of King David, and Isaiah's prophecy concerning him – 'There shall come forth a rod out of the stem of Jesse, and a Branch shall grow out of his roots, and the spirit of the Lord shall rest upon him' (Isaiah 11.1–2) – was interpreted by Christians as referring to Jesus, who was

Opposite: *A Green Man with the Virgin Mary on a corbel in the choir of the Cathedral of St Peter, Exeter, Devon. Before 1309. Photo: Ruth Wylie. Reproduced by kind permission of the Dean and Chapter of Exeter.*

supposedly descended from David (see Matthew 1.1–17 and Luke 2.4). The theme of the Tree of Jesse became popular in sacred art, including stained-glass windows and illustrations in psalters, from the eleventh century onwards. The Legend of the True Cross would provide a suitable companion image as it too is a tale of a prophecy concerning a tree which was fulfilled in Christ.

Exeter Cathedral is by no means the only site where foliate heads appear in apparent association with the Virgin Mary. Indeed, when searching for Green Men in a cathedral, we should always examine the roof-bosses in the Lady Chapel as well as in the nave and the cloisters. The mid-fourteenth-century Lady Chapel of Ely Cathedral has several foliate heads while in Sheffield Cathedral there are foliate heads disgorging trees rather than mere leaves or twigs, and even a figure which could be interpreted as giving birth to a tree! Above her is a Lamb holding a banner with a cross upon it – the symbols of the risen, victorious Christ – and behind the Lamb is a sapling.

Curiously enough, this image echoes the woman – upside down and also seemingly giving birth to a tree – depicted on a seal excavated at Harappa in the Indus Valley and dating from around 2000 BC! [Marshall 1931 Vol.1: 52; Campbell 1962 (1991: 166)].

The only other remotely comparable Christian image of which I am aware is to be found in the Cathedral of St Bertrand de Comminges, in the Haute Garonne.

Here, in the choir-stalls (completed towards the middle of the sixteenth century and displaying several foliate heads), there is a misericord with the figure of a harpy – an unpleasant, predatory creature from Greek mythology, with the head and breasts of a woman, and the wings and feet of a bird, usually a vulture – apparently giving birth to a leaf-mask. Or could the sculptor have intended it as a fig-leaf? Maybe the Sheffield figure is not giving birth but doing acrobatics on an upturned tree stump. We cannot be too careful about jumping to conclusions!

The temptation to jump to conclusions could, indeed, be strong for the Green Man enthusiast who comes for the first time, unprepared, upon a 'lily-crucifixion', such as the one in a stained-glass window (c.1450) in St Michael's at the North Gate, in Oxford. Could this be a 'green' Christ, arising from a plant, with His arms metamorphosing into leaves and flowers? On closer inspection, the viewer will see that this is not the case. Christ is quite separate from the plant – a Madonna lily (*Lilium candidum*) – but is nailed to it. Images of Christ crucified on a lily plant in full bloom occur both in English and Continental churches. In some, as in the painting on the

An intriguing roof-boss of the Lady Chapel in the Cathedral of SS Peter and Paul, Sheffield. Fifteenth century. Photo Ruth Wylie. Reproduced by kind permission of the Administrator of Sheffield Cathedral.

ceiling of St Helen's, Abingdon, in Oxfordshire (1391), there is no cross at all, and Christ hangs directly from the branching plant. In others, there is a shadowy cross behind the lily. Sometimes the 'lily cross' grows out of a beautiful pot or urn. Lilies, either in pots or in the hand of Gabriel, first appear in representations of the Annunciation at the beginning of the fourteenth century. This offers a clue to the origin of 'lily crucifixions'. Mediaeval Christians believed that the Annunciation and Crucifixion both took place on March 25. Catholic tradition sees Mary as mediatrix and co-redemptrix with her Son by reason of her co-operation in the process of Redemption. The combination of Mary's lily with the Cross of Christ would have made perfect sense to ordinary mediaeval Christians, whose ever-increasing devotion to the Blessed Virgin prompted Pope Sixtus IV to proclaim the first official feast of the Immaculate Conception in 1476 [Rogers 1997].

An influential mediaeval book which fuelled interest in the Virgin Mary as a co-redemptrix was *Meditationes Vitae Christi* (Meditations on the Life of Christ), written early in the fourteenth century by a Franciscan whose identity has not been established. The book is based on the New Testament but includes material from apocryphal literature, and even from the author's imagination, to fill out the stories of the Crucifixion and Mary's experiences and sufferings, so as to make them appear more vivid and more moving. This book was partly responsible for the popularity of the continental chapels for meditation mentioned earlier in this chapter.

For some Christian theologians, such as Rabanus Maurus (780–856), rank vegetation served as a metaphor for sins of the flesh. Certain types of Green Man, especially the more horrific, half-suffocated ones, may have been inspired by the writings of these theologians rather than by the legends of Adam and Seth. However, like all the other clues which we have found, such a conclusion offers only a partial explanation.

The Bible itself has many references to leaves, branches and other greenery that can be found with the aid of a Concordance. Some of these references indeed associate vegetation with the wicked, such as the passage in Ezekiel (8.17), which Rabanus Maurus cites. Here God says of those who worship false gods 'Lo, they put the branch to their nose.' In Isaiah 14.19, Lucifer is told 'thou are cast out of thy grave like an abominable branch'. Advice given in the Apocrypha (Ecclesiasticus 6.3) may also have inspired some foliate heads: 'Extol not thyself in the counsel of thy heart; that

*A Green Man roof-boss in the Lady Chapel of the Cathedral of SS
Peter and Paul, Sheffield. Fifteenth century. Photos: Ruth Wylie.
Reproduced by kind permission of the Administrator of
Sheffield Cathedral.*

thy soul be not torn in pieces as a bull [staying alone]. Thou shalt eat
up thy leaves, and lose thy fruit and leave thyself as a dry tree.'

However, like so many other symbols, vegetation can have more
than one meaning, even in the Bible. Here, there are also plenty of
passages in which leaves and trees are associated with the Righteous.
In Psalm 1, for example, we read 'And he shall be like a tree planted
by the rivers of water, that bringeth forth his fruit in season; his leaf
also shall not wither and whatsoever he doeth shall flourish'. A
similar passage occurs in Jeremiah 17.8 concerning the man who
trusts in the Lord. In contrast to Lucifer, who is to be cast out as an
abominable branch, 'the righteous shall flourish like a branch',
according to Proverbs 11.28. Perhaps, some Green Men were
intended to make worshippers meditate on the choice between the
fate of righteous and unrighteous vegetation.

As for those foliate heads whose tongues protrude, they may
well represent a reminder of the need to govern the tongue,

A poppy-head in the choir-stalls of the church of St Mary, Beverley, East Yorkshire. 1445. Photo: Ruth Wylie.

described by James in the third chapter of his Epistle as 'a fire, a world of iniquity... an unruly evil, full of deadly poison.' A double tongue was the sign of a sinner and malefactor (Ecclesiasticus 5.9 and 14). There are, however, plenty of heads whose tongues protrude but which are free of greenery, so this may not be the whole explanation.

Unfortunately, little can be concluded with any certainty. We have discovered a series of circumstances and ideas that could explain the significance of some Gothic foliate heads, but we have not discovered a single, unifying concept common to them all.

Green Men, especially the disgorging variety, reached their pinnacle of diversity during the Gothic Age, but they go back even further. In the next chapter we shall make the acquaintance of their ancestors in Romanesque churches and elsewhere.

6: THE ROMANESQUE AGE AND ITS FOLIATE HEADS

Unlike us, Green Men appear to be descended from monstrous cats! That, at any rate, is the impression given by the majority of foliate heads dating from the Romanesque period. Humanoid heads are not totally absent, but the typical Romanesque foliate head is distinctly feline and disgorges long tangled stems, with little in the way of leaves. Often the stems are decorated with bead-like dots, and there may also be stylized flowers and motifs resembling fir-cones. In comparison with their Gothic descendants, Romanesque foliate heads show greater uniformity of design. They also have a more limited habitat, and are most likely to be seen on the carved capitals of columns or near doorways.

'Romanesque' is the term used for the style of art and architecture prevalent in Europe from the tenth to the twelfth century. In England the architectural style is also known as 'Norman' because it was introduced to this country around 1066. As its name suggests, Romanesque architecture was partially inspired by Roman buildings, but, in some places, it absorbed certain Byzantine and Arabic elements as well. The main characteristics of Romanesque architecture are round arches and massive masonry, which produce an atmosphere of sombre grandeur. Decoration is often sparse, but, when present, it is highly imaginative, displaying a love for the fantastic and grotesque, including foliate heads.

Some historical background

The year 800 is generally seen as the beginning of a new era in European history. For centuries, Western Europe had been troubled by barbarian incursions and civil strife that inhibited trade and led to a decline in the importance of once flourishing towns. On Christmas Day 800, after a long and ultimately successful struggle to consolidate his power and authority, Charlemagne, king of the Franks since 768, was crowned Emperor by his ally, Pope Leo III.

Claiming legitimate succession to the Roman Empire, Charlemagne proceeded to create a highly efficient administrative system and to lay the foundations of what became known as the Frankish, or Holy Roman, Empire. This Empire was conceived as a united Christian realm, whose Emperor, crowned by the Pope, was God's temporal Vicar on Earth, with the responsibility to protect the

A corbel in the transepts of the Liebfrauenkirche, Trier, Germany. 1235. These heads share stylistic similarities with those re-cycled by Archbishop Nicetius as well as those now in the city's Rheinisches Landesmuseum. Photo: Ruth Wylie.

Church – a duty which he interpreted as giving him the right to take the lead in all Church affairs, including the appointment of bishops.

During the centuries of confusion and instability most building projects had been modest in size and executed in wood but the establishment of a new Empire under Charlemagne brought a revival of monumental construction in stone on a scale unseen since Roman times. Both the Church and the Monarchy felt the need for buildings whose size and magnificence would reflect their God-given authority.

Charlemagne abandoned the tradition according to which the Frankish Court was peripatetic, constantly moving from one 'capital' to another on royal progress. He chose to settle at Aachen, where he built a royal palace, taking his inspiration from the Lateran in Rome, said to have been the palace of the Emperor Constantine, who had presented it to the Church. Adjoining the palace in Aachen was the imperial Palatine Chapel that incorporated classical columns brought on Charlemagne's instructions from Ravenna. The sixth-century church of San Vitale in the same city was one of the models for the Chapel.

Charlemagne also extended his generous patronage to the building, or reconstruction, of a number of churches including that dedicated to St Riquier in the monastery at Centula, near Abbeville. Centula's energetic abbot, Angibert, was a personal friend of the Emperor and a major luminary at Court, where he was known as 'Homer'. Charlemagne provided both money and specialized craftsmen to work on the church. He even sent to Rome itself for bases, columns and mouldings, which were brought to Centula at great expense, to enhance the beauty of the enormous new monastic church.

Charlemagne was not the first to recycle 'pagan' artifacts to beautify a Christian church. Three centuries earlier, Archbishop Nicetius of Trier (Germany) had raided the portico of a nearby Roman temple dating from the reign of Hadrian (117–38 AD) and known as Am Herrenbrünnchen. His activities are of interest to Green Man enthusiasts because what he took from the temple included several leaf-masks. These he caused to be placed on four pillars at the crossing of the cathedral built under his direction during the sixth century. The heads, which wear crowns of leaves, are human in appearance, with fairly normal features, apart from the flattish foliage which covers the forehead and cheeks as though it were pasted on. Although these leaf-masks were not purpose-made, they represent one of the earliest known instances of Green Men inside a Christian church.

These leaf-masks remained clearly on view in the centre of the cathedral for some five hundred years, until masonry erected during the great rebuilding programme of the eleventh century hid them from public view. They were rediscovered in the course of restoration work during the nineteenth century, when a plaster cast was made of one of the leaf-masks (now in the Rheinische Landesmuseum in Trier). The link with Am Herrenbrünnchen was established after a detailed examination of the stone during further restoration in 1961–3, when a small window was inserted into the screening masonry to enable visitors to view one of the masks *in situ*.

We can only guess at the bishop's reasons for removing the masks from the temple to so central a place in his new House of God. Perhaps he was simply trying to reduce the cost to the diocese by

The font in the church of St Mary, Luppitt, Devon. Twelfth century.
Photo: Ruth Wylie.

utilizing existing decorative material. Or, maybe, he was hoping to recapture something of the prestige that Trier had enjoyed in Roman times.

Attitudes towards the classical world had been gradually changing as it became more remote in time. The early Christians had rejected everything that smacked of paganism, including even wreaths and garlands, and many centuries had to elapse before the rose lost its association with Roman orgies and was rehabilitated as a symbol of the Virgin Mary that gave its name to the rosary. By Charlemagne's time, the image of ancient Rome as a city of debauched heathens had given way to a new vision of a civilized city at the centre of an Empire where law and order prevailed.

Charlemagne's Palatine Chapel has survived to this day, and although Saint-Riquier was destroyed quite early on, its innovative architecture provided the pattern for many future Romanesque churches. In particular, its impressive size and numerous soaring towers established monumental proportions and vertical tendencies that were in complete contrast to the smaller, more horizontally aligned churches of earlier Christian communities.

Charlemagne was also a keen patron of learning and the arts, who summoned to his Court scholars, artisans, architects and other craftsmen from all over Europe, and encouraged the copying of manuscripts. Eminent teachers from places as far apart as England, Ireland, Lombardy and Spain, taught at the royal school which, on Charlemagne's insistence, was attended not only by his own sons but

*A capital in the nave of the church of St Peter, Northampton.
Twelfth century. Photo: Ruth Wylie. Reproduced by kind permission
of the Churches Conservation Trust.*

also by those of his nobles. Among the teachers was Alcuin of York -
a city whose cathedral then boasted a fine library and a school which
taught grammar, rhetoric, law, poetry, natural history, arithmetic and
geometry, as well as the Scriptures and methods of calculating the
date of Easter.

Now that pagan Rome had become a distant memory,
superceded by early Christian Rome, the creators of the new Empire
regarded the cultural history of both Romes as a source of pride and
a model to be emulated. Four hundred years earlier, St Jerome had
been seriously troubled lest his immortal soul be endangered by his
fondness for the writers of classical antiquity. Carolingian scholars,
including Alcuin of York (who was well acquainted with the writings
of such pagan authors as Virgil and Ovid) no longer had any qualms
of that kind, although these authors were often re-interpreted from a
Christian standpoint. Indeed, many classical works have survived
into modern times thanks to the activities of Carolingian scribes.

Charlemagne died in 814 but, under his successors, his Empire
failed to maintain its strength and unity. This was in part because of
Viking, Magyar and Saracen invasions, and also because of the
Frankish custom of dividing property, including kingdoms, between
the surviving sons. After decades of turmoil and confusion, order was
restored under the Saxon Emperors, Henry I (919–36) and his son,
Otto the Great. The latter was crowned King of Germany in

Charlemagne's capital at Aachen in 936 and in the following year, he was crowned Emperor in Rome.

However, the Empire over which Otto ruled was greatly reduced in size in comparison with that of Charlemagne, who had controlled most of western Europe apart from Spain and Portugal (these had been largely under Moorish rule since 711). The western half of the Empire had irrevocably gone its own way and was evolving into what is now France. At the time much of the territory was composed of semi-independent feudal duchies, such as Anjou, Aquitaine and Toulouse. Normandy had been formally ceded to the Vikings who, as settled Normans, soon became as enthusiastic about building as they had once been about sacking and destroying. Thus, the eastern half of the Empire over which Otto and subsequent 'Emperors of the Romans' ruled consisted of little more than the German principalities and Austria, and at times adjacent territories, including the Netherlands and northern Italy.

The detailed history of the two parts of Charlemagne's former Empire during the subsequent two hundred years does not concern us here. What matters is that the Christian religion continued to be the dominant influence in the lives of everyone from Emperor to peasant, while the monumental style of church building pioneered at Centula was emulated in a renewed frenzy of construction.

The rise of monasteries

Monasteries played a central role in the lives of mediaeval communities, and the eleventh and twelfth centuries were the Golden Age of monasticism. Most of the enormous Romanesque churches were built to serve the needs of both resident monks and the constant stream of lay folk that flocked to the monasteries as pilgrims, guests or supplicants. In the monasteries, kings and nobles were entertained by the abbots; the poor received charity from the almoners, and the sick were treated by the infirmarers. Mediaeval monasteries were not merely religious foundations, but also performed many of the functions that today belong to hotels, social services, hospitals, schools and universities.

The words 'monk' and 'monastery' ultimately derive from the Greek *monos*, meaning 'alone', and the first Christian monks were people who withdrew from the world to live solitary lives in quiet, even desolate, places, in caves or huts, where they could pray and meditate in peace. Such were the so-called 'Desert Fathers', who lived lives of extreme asceticism in the deserts of Egypt. During the fourth century, some began to group their separate huts into

*A capital in the former abbey church of St Austremoine, Issoire,
Puy-de-Dôme, Auvergne. Twelfth century. Photo: Ruth Wylie.*

communities, or even to live in communal dwellings under the
guidance of an abbot – a term derived from the Aramaic word for
'father'.

The movement towards an ever more structured way of life for
monks reached an important landmark in the early sixth century,
when St Benedict (c.480–c.550) established the monastery of Monte
Cassino in Italy, and drew up a Rule which became the basis of
monasticism in the Western Empire. The next development was
towards greater centralization, initiated by St Benedict of Aniane
(c.750–821), abbot of a monastery in Languedoc, who brought most
of the monastic houses in Charlemagne's empire under a single
authority. His ideas were revived in the tenth century when, in 932,
Abbot Odo of Cluny received permission from the Pope to found
daughter-houses governed, not by their own abbots, but by priors
answerable to the Abbot of Cluny. Odo was also empowered to
reform existing Benedictine monasteries and make them subordinate
to Cluny.

The monastery at Cluny was founded in 910 on land in
Burgundy donated for the purpose by William, Duke of Aquitaine

and Marquis of Gothia. Its foundation charter granted it exemption from all ecclesiastical and lay interference, other than that of the Pope in the unlikely event that the house became seriously disordered. At the height of its power, Cluny controlled more than a thousand other Benedictine monastic houses.

The growing prestige of Cluny led to the rebuilding of its church twice within two hundred years, each time on a more magnificent scale. The final version, known to modern writers as Cluny III and begun in 1086, was largely destroyed at the time of the French Revolution, but an idea of the splendour of its fabulous decoration can be gained from other surviving monastic churches, such as those at Vézelay and Moissac, which were influenced by the example of Cluny. The great size and the lavish ornamentation of the Cluniac churches were matched by the pomp of the elaborate processions and services conducted in them, and by the beauty of the Gregorian chant, which was heard to perfect advantage under their barrel-vaulted stone roofs.

Although the original intention of monks was to isolate themselves from the world in order to devote themselves to God, those who built the great Romanesque monasteries formed an important element in the society of their day. Towns and commerce still played so minor a role that they were ignored by contemporaries, such as Adalbero, Bishop of Laon (France), who, writing in the 1020s, expressed the belief (referred to in the previous chapter) that God had ordained the division of his Church on Earth into three harmonious, interdependent categories: those who prayed, those who fought and defended the Church, and those who laboured. This static view of society reflected the prevailing feudal system by which a privileged class was granted land and the income produced by the peasants living on it in return for military service when required, or, in the case of religious foundations, in return for their prayers.

All three categories were devoutly Christian and preoccupied to the point of obsession with those aspects of their religion relating to the transitory nature of life on Earth, death, life after death, and divine judgement. The concept of Hell had been inherited by Christianity from Judaism, but did not loom large in the thinking of either the Jews or the early Christians. For the latter, the important thing was that, through Christ, they could be saved and enter Heaven. Gradually, however, the emphasis changed, and, by the end of the twelfth century, mediaeval Christians feared Hell more than they looked forward to Heaven.

A Tree of Life in the tympanum of the south doorway of the church of St Olave, Fritwell, Oxfordshire. Photo: Ruth Wylie.

Two books, in particular, helped to fuel this fear. One was the *Dialogues* attributed to Pope Gregory I (590–604), which included an account of the punishments that the wicked would suffer after death. The other was the *Vision of St Paul* by an unknown fourth-century writer, which likewise contained a terrifying description of Hell. St Augustine of Hippo (354–430) had dismissed the *Vision* as false but, being horrific, it continued to attract fascinated attention. Between 800 and 1300 it was repeatedly copied; its ideas were popularized in sermons, and probably influenced Dante's description of Hell and Purgatory [Chadwick 1995: 136]. As a result people were afraid, not so much of dying *per se* as of dying before they had had time to repent of their sins and make amends before facing their Maker. This preoccupation with death and damnation was reflected in the awesome scenes of Christ in Majesty and the Last Judgement placed over the portals of many Romanesque churches, and in the lurid images of vice and sin carved on the capitals of their naves.

The monastic life was seen as the most authentic and complete interpretation of the Christian ideal, and entering a monastery as the surest way to salvation. Monarchs and rich men could wipe out their sins and gain rewards in Heaven by founding a monastic house, or by giving land to an existing one, while a knight could save his soul, by participating in wars against the Moors in Spain, or by becoming a Crusader in the Holy Land.

121

The ordinary laity believed that crumbs of salvation fell from monastic tables and that the whole community benefited from the presence and prayers of the monks. Monasteries were regarded as citadels of spiritual power and Divine Grace, able to combat and hold at bay the Evil One, who 'as a roaring lion, walketh about, seeking whom he may devour' (1 Peter 5:8). Just by being there, with their ceaseless services and intercession, the monasteries appeared to offer comfort and protection to ordinary people. The prayers of the spiritually privileged assumed even greater significance with the development, during the eleventh century, of the doctrine of Purgatory – a place where souls neither sufficiently good to enter Heaven immediately, nor sufficiently evil to be damned for all eternity, underwent a process of purging and purification, which could be shortened or mitigated through the saying of special masses on behalf of the departed.

The importance of pilgrimages

For the laity, especially the poor, one of the chief means of atoning for sins, seeking cures, and obtaining spiritual merit was to make a pilgrimage to one or more of the many shrines now situated throughout Christendom and the Holy Land. At the same time, the cult of saints' relics developed into a major feature of mediaeval Christianity, as people came to believe in their miraculous powers and in the role of the departed saints as celestial advocates, able to plead before the throne of God on behalf of repentant sinners. Every monastery and cathedral strove to acquire as many relics as possible in order to gain prestige and to attract pilgrims seeking to enlist the aid of the saints in question.

In mediaeval times, to undertake a pilgrimage as a penance was not necessarily to get off lightly. Travelling was slow, arduous and exceedingly hazardous. The risks of falling ill, being robbed, or even killed, were great. The pilgrimage monasteries acted as staging-posts, providing shelter, succour, and the possibility of meeting up with other pilgrims to form larger groups more able to cope with bandits, accidents and other perils.

The cult of relics and the popular enthusiasm for pilgrimages influenced the architecture of churches in several ways. The need to give large numbers of people access to the shrines without disrupting the devotions and daily routine of the monks led to such developments as the raising of the choir above the crypt in which the relics were housed, the provision of aisles on either side of the nave, and the inclusion of an ambulatory around the apse.

Feline heads on the lid of the tomb of Gundrada (died 1085), wife of William de Warenne, who received Lewes from William the Conqueror. From a cast in the Sussex Archaeological Museum, Barbican House, Lewes. The original, made of Tournai marble, is in the church of St John, Southover, where the Warennes founded the Priory of St Pancras. Twelfth century. Photo: Ruth Wylie. Reproduced by kind permission of the Sussex Archaeological Museum, Barbican House, Lewes.

In this age of faith and fear of damnation, of pilgrimage and monastic zeal, of colossal expenditure on the construction of churches intended to reflect the splendour of Heaven, sculpture became an important means of teaching and bringing home the Christian messages and Christian virtues to monks and lay pilgrims alike. Few of the latter could read and, for these, pictures in stone took the place of books. What is particularly relevant to our explorations is that new sculptural motifs travelled, like souvenirs, along the pilgrimage routes. Most of the facilities along these routes were provided by the Cluniac Order, which was then foremost in the building and reconstruction of monastic houses and churches. This uniformity favoured the copying and rapid spread of motifs which found favour with the Order and its benefactors. Among these motifs was the disgorging foliate head, which, at this time, makes its first appearance as a popular and accepted motif throughout Western Christendom.

123

The Holy Places of Jerusalem were, of course, the major goal for pilgrims (Chaucer's Wife of Bath had been there no less than three times), but not all could afford either the time or the money necessary for the journey, and there were also periods when circumstances made access difficult or impossible. In 637 Jerusalem was captured by the Muslims, who themselves regarded the city as sacred. The Crusaders gained possession of it in 1099, but it was again lost to the Muslims less than a century later, in 1197. There were, however, many other places of pilgrimage, among them Santiago de Compostela, in Galicia, northern Spain (indeed, the Wife of Bath had been there too!).

The most northerly parts of Spain, bordering on the Pyrenees, had never been fully conquered by the Moors following their invasion of the peninsula in 711. After Charles Martel had halted the Moorish advance into the Frankish Kingdom in 732, Christian nobles who had fled into the Asturian mountains came down and established a small kingdom, which became the bridgehead for the long, slow reconquest of Spain, The capital of the kingdom was first Oviedo and then León. Following the discovery, early in the ninth century, of the supposed tomb of the Apostle James (according to legend by a peasant led to a field by a shining star), a shrine was built on the site. Santiago de Compostela (St James of the Starry Field) became the most famous city of the new Christian realm, and the most important place of pilgrimage after Rome and Jerusalem.

From all over Europe, people flocked to the shrine of St James, and many of the great Romanesque churches and monasteries were built along the routes taken by pilgrims. One route came from the north-east Channel coast, via Amiens, Paris-St Denis (where it was joined by pilgrims from Laon and Reims), Orleans, Tours (where pilgrims from Chartres joined the route), Poitiers, Saint-Jean-d'Angély, Saintes, Bordeaux, and Dax to Roncevalles, where it converged with a second route coming from Troyes and Langres, via Vézelay, La Charité-sur-Loire, Chateauroux, Neuvy-Saint-Sepulcre, Saint-Léonard-de-Noblat, Limoges, Périgueux, and Saint-Sever, and a third, coming from Clermont-Ferrand, Cluny and Lyon, via Le Puy, Conques, Rocamadour, Cahors and Moissac. From Roncevalles all the pilgrims from all three directions proceeded to Puente la Reina (south of Pamploma). Here they met up with pilgrims coming along the fourth main route: from Germany, via Luzern, Berne, Lucerne, Genf, Chambéry, Valence, Montelimar, Nîmes, Saint-Gille-du-Gard (the junction for travellers from Fréjus on the Mediterranean, Aix-en-Provence, and Arles), Montpellier, Narbonne, Carcassonne,

A boss under the entrance archway to the Chapter House of the Abbaye St Georges, St Martin-de-Boscherville, Seine Maritime, Normandy. Twelfth century. Photo: Ruth Wylie.

Toulouse, Lescar, Puerto de Somport and Jaca. All the pilgrims then took the same route: via Estella, Longroño, Najera, Burgos, Castrogeriz, Frómista, Carrion de los Condes, Sahagún, León, Astorga, and Villafranca del Bierzo, to their common destination at Santiago de Compostela near the Atlantic coast.

Romanesque sculpture as a whole
If you are a Green Man spotter, your first, if not only, concern on arriving at a church is to track down and record every foliate head. That is fine, if your curiosity stops there. If, however, you are a Green Man explorer, intent on trying to understand the motif, you will need to consider the whole context of Romanesque imagery and the company that the Green Men keep.

125

The typically cat-faced foliate head is just one of many unusual images to be seen in a Romanesque church. Most are just as strange, or even stranger than the Green Men.

The people of the eleventh and twelfth centuries were curious, impressionable, and fearful of the Devil. They wanted to know what Heaven and Hell were like, and how they could reach the former and avoid the latter. They were as fascinated by fabulous beasts, composite monsters, and half-humans, as today's children are by dinosaurs and aliens.

Popular curiosity about strange creatures was both satisfied and whetted by various books of the period, among them early bestiaries. Few people possessed or had direct access to such books, but those who did were often the patrons of sculptors and referred to them when commissioning work. Translated into stone carvings visible to all, extracts from these books achieved the mediaeval equivalent of mass circulation, and were never 'out of print'!

One rich source of inspiration for sculptors in search of fabulous beasts was the *Etymologies*, or *Origines*, of St Isidore of Seville (c.560–636), who believed that Christian lessons could be learnt even from the appearance and behaviour of monsters. Our word 'monster' is derived from the Latin *monere*, meaning 'to warn', and originally denoted a 'divine portent'. For the theologian John Scotus Erigena (c.815–77) pictorial representation was the highest form of perception, and beauty the perfect expression of being. In his view, art could bring the soul closer to salvation, and even flawed beauty and the deformities of demons and monsters could encourage the believer to seek the absolute beauty of God.

Another source for the sculptor was the *Speculum Ecclesiae* (c.1090–1120) by Honorius Augustodunensis, a monk who worked in Canterbury and Germany, but was known as Honorius of Autun although his connections with that town are unknown. *Speculum Ecclesiae* is a book of sermons which systematically explore parallels between the Old and New Testaments, making use of examples - often very farfetched – from the animal kingdom to confirm the fulfilment of the former in the latter.

Among the beasts described by St Isidore was the griffin, which had an eagle's head and a lion's body, and was reputed to guard a hoard of gold and emeralds in Scythia – a distant and, by then, largely mythical land. Many tales were told about these allegedly ferocious and powerful beasts, in whom most people implicitly believed. King Robert the Pious of France (996–1031) possessed a 'griffin's egg' (it was probably an ostrich egg), enclosed in a silver

A capital on the chancel arch in the church of St Michael and All Angels, Sutton, Cambridgeshire. Twelfth century. Photo: Ruth Wylie.

case, and even made people of lesser rank swear oaths upon it. Hildegard of Bingen (1098–1179) was sufficiently interested in the creature to collect information about it and its eggs, and she reached somewhat negative conclusions about its nature and its usefulness [Cherry 1995: 84; 859]. In general, this was the prevailing view, and stories about griffins were often the starting point for homilies against greed.

Another fabulous composite beast from the East was the manticore. In classical times, this was purported to come from Persia. It was given new life in mediaeval bestiaries. The creature's name is a corruption of a Persian term meaning 'man-eater'. Manticores were said to have the head of a man, the body of a lion, three rows of teeth in each jaw, and poisoned spines on their tails. Its ferocity and fleetness of foot led to its being associated in mediaeval times with Satan, who went about chasing and feeding on men's souls. A manticore, ridden by a horned devil, appears on the capital in the

A capital in the Chapelle de St Saturnin, St Wandrille, Seine Maritime, Normandy. Possibly recovered from an older Carolingian building on the site. Photo: Ruth Wylie.

crypt of Canterbury Cathedral, where its neighbours include other fantastic creatures, such as a two-headed wolf-woman; an amphisbaena (a kind of lizard with a head at each end); a wyvern (a two-legged, winged dragon, that was, among other things, the emblem of the Saxon Kings of Wessex, including Alfred, and can be seen on one of the English banners in the Bayeux Tapestry); a disgorging 'cat-face', and several more ordinary creatures playing musical instruments.

With an appetite no less insatiable than that of the manticore, the builders of churches ransacked every possible source – bestiaries, fables, Moslem and Christian manuscripts, the art forms of past cultures, local legends, and even patterns (including fabulous oriental beasts) woven into the luxury brocades and other textiles imported from the East to be made into altar cloths and church vestments - for ideas which would impress the worshipper with the wonders of God's creation and warn him against sin and the wiles of the Devil.

The idea of transferring images from manuscripts to carving on the exterior of churches for the edification of worshippers may have come from Oliba, Abbot of Ripoll, or one of his circle. Ripoll (some fifty miles north of Barcelona) was then a major centre of learning which, in 1046, had two hundred and forty-six volumes in its library [Conant 1973: 94]. From about 950 onwards monks in the Abbey's scriptorium were busy producing manuscripts whose iconography is reflected in the elaborately decorated west portal of their church of Santa Maria (c.1020–30) [illustration in Toman 1997: 295].

The inspiration for mediaeval illustrated manuscripts came from many sources, including Byzantine, Roman, Islamic, Celtic, Norse

A nave capital in the church of St Peter, Northampton. Twelfth
century. Photo: Ruth Wylie. Reproduced by kind permission of the
Churches Conservation Trust.

and Anglo-Saxon art. Latin was then the *lingua franca* of all literate
persons, mainly monks, so that scholars and manuscripts could travel
throughout Western Christendom and still be understood. Alcuin of
York, for example, was able to teach at the court of Charlemagne and
to oversee the work in the scriptorium at Tours, where he was abbot
from 756 to 804. From the sixth century onwards, Irish monks were
travelling through France, Italy and Germany, founding monasteries
and scriptoria, among them Luxeuil (Haute Saône, France) in 590,
Bobbio (halfway between Genoa and Piacenza, Italy) in 613, and
St Gall (south of Lake Constance in Switzerland) in 614. The
interlacing ribbons, curling foliage, and tiny, often inconsequential,
heads typical of ornamentation in the Book of Durrow (c.680), the
Lindisfarne Gospels (c.695), and the Book of Kells (end of the eighth
century), appear in manuscripts all over Europe.

Many of the great Romanesque churches had vivid
representations of set pieces from the Apocalypse, such as Christ in
Majesty and the Last Judgement, carved in stone in the tympana
above church porches. Here the Righteous can be seen at the right
hand of Christ with the saints and angels, while sinners are being

*Foliate female exhibitionist by the south entrance to the church of
SS Michael and Mary, Melbourne, Derbyshire.
Photo: Mercia MacDermott.*

shoved and jostled into the mouth of Hell to His left, where demons
and monsters eagerly await them.

Such representations first appeared in Catalonia during the early
eleventh century, under the influence of illustrations from the popular
and much copied commentary on the Apocalypse by Beatus, Abbot
of Liébana (in northern Spain, south-west of Santander), who died in
798. The earliest surviving example of such sculpture is a lintel in the
church of Saint-Genis-des-Fontaines (some forty miles north-east of
Ripoll) dated 1020–21 [Conant 1973: 64], and the most spectacular
is above the south portal of the former abbey church of Saint Pierre in
Moissac (1120–35).

In mediaeval times, church portals were not simply places where
worshippers entered and left a church. They were often also the place
where trials, both secular and ecclesiastical, were held, where
judgements were given, where oaths were sworn and where
marriages were solemnized. Depictions of the Last Judgement and
other solemn scenes were particularly appropriate in a place used for
such important events. In addition, figures of guardian lions were
often placed on either side of the entrance, in imitation of those said

A combined Green Man and female exhibitionist on a pillar at the crossing under the tower of the church of SS Michael and Mary, Melbourne, Derbyshire. Twelfth century. The church was built as an alternative court for the Bishop of Carlisle when raids by the Scots made that city too dangerous. Photo: Ruth Wylie.

to stand by the throne of Solomon, who was famed for his wise and just judgements. People seeking sanctuary in churches were often considered to be immune from arrest once they had grasped the ring of the knocker on the portal.

Great imagination also went into carving images to warn worshippers of the sins and vices which would result in their being in the wrong place on the Day of Judgement. During the eleventh and twelfth centuries, the main builders of churches were the monastic orders, bound by vows of poverty and chastity, and convinced to the point of fanaticism that women were instruments of Satan and that any form of sexuality was a sin.

The Romanesque churches built by misogynist monks abound with images of lust intended to portray all sexual activity as abhorrent and to warn of the divine punishment which awaited those who yielded to temptation. There are megaphallic and ithyphallic males; men whose penises are being attacked by reptiles; exhibitionist women exposing their vulvas; women who appear to be suckling snakes; and almost every form of indecent exposure and sexual symbol that can be imagined – all designed to disgust, frighten and deter. Even the grotesque heads on corbels which pull faces and stick out their tongues could have been intended to carry a sexual message, since the tongue often had phallic connotations. Thus, those figures who are using their fingers to stretch their mouths may be making a gesture analogous to that of the female exhibitionists who are pulling open their vulvas. They might equally be a reference to the verses in Isaiah 57, which say: 'But draw hither, ye sons of the sorceress, the seed of the adulterer and the whore. Against whom do you sport yourselves? Against whom make ye a wide mouth and draw out the tongue?'

Of these images, the female exhibitionists are of particular interest to Green Man explorers, because there are churches where the two images are combined, or in close proximity. One such example is the twelfth-century church of St Michael and St Mary in Melbourne, Derbyshire. Here, on a capital at the crossing, a female 'cat-face' both disgorges foliage and displays its private parts, while on a capital at the south portal there is a female exhibitionist whose arms end in foliage.

Female figures showing their genitalia can be found in the art of many different cultures throughout the ages, although their purpose and significance may not always be the same. Some Maori *hei tiki*, for example, were carved as overtly female figures displaying their genitalia, and were intended as talismans to ensure fertility and easy childbirth. In many traditions, both male and female genitalia are believed, by reason of their life-giving function, to have apotropaic (protective) properties [Jones 2002: 248–52].

The Romanesque female exhibitionist is often erroneously thought to be part of this ancient tradition of images and symbols promoting fertility and offering protection. The popular name for this image – Sheela-na-gig – is a corruption of an Irish term for a loose woman, and was introduced during the nineteenth century by folklorists who believed that the image was originally an ancient Irish talisman to encourage fertility.

The Romanesque 'Sheela', however, tends to be frantic in gesture and repulsive in appearance, and lacks such qualities as an impressive physique, beauty, repose and gravity, one or more of which generally characterize other magical and ritual images. Research by Jørgen Andersen [1977] and Anthony Weir and James Jerman [1986] indicates that, far from being a fertility goddess, the female exhibitionist is an *anti*-fertility image intended to arouse disgust in the beholder and to foster the idea that sex is sordid and sinful. Moreover, although 'Sheelas' are, indeed, widespread in Ireland, they came there (and to England) from Spain and south-west France, via the pilgrim routes to and from Santiago de Compostela. In churches all along the routes taken by pilgrims, female exhibitionists

Sheela-na-gig on the corbel table of the Romanesque church at Kilpeck, Herefordshire. Photo: Bob Trubshaw.

appear as one of the many types of grotesque, intentionally shocking, and repellant images carved to deter the beholder from yielding to such sins as lust and avarice.

In time, the original message of the female exhibitionists was forgotten, and, from being one of many images warning against the sins of lust and debauchery, they came to be seen by some women as talismans against childlessness. Some images show signs of rubbing, as though their aid had been invoked. Their presence on late mediaeval secular buildings, such as castles, both in Ireland and England suggests that, despite the efforts to make them appear edifyingly repellant, the exhibitionists eventually became confused in the popular mind with the ancient tradition of apotropaic sexual images and gestures. 'Sheelas' on secular buildings are more common in Ireland than in England, where, however, they are not altogether absent. The gateway of the castle of Tickhill, Yorkshire is protected not only by a 'Sheela', but also by a phallic male figure, both of which are now in a poor condition and hard to see.

The idea of placing earthy or even sexually explicit images in a church may strike us as peculiar in the extreme, accustomed as we are to associate churches with enhanced decorum and good behaviour. We might well be tempted to conclude that some irreverent mason had played a joke or cocked a snook at his venerable and pious employers. The position of 'rude' images, if nothing else, should convince us that this could not be the case. Most of them occur on doorways, porches, corbels and capitals clearly visible from ground level, and doubtless those who were financing the construction monitored both its overall growth (and cost!) and such details as the carvings.

The decoration of mediaeval churches was no more arbitrary or haphazard than the words of the sermons preached therein, and carvings were intended to be didactic and to provide a visual reminder of the teachings and admonishments received from the clergy. Even those carvings which appear to us to be fanciful or amusing may well have had a serious meaning for the mediaeval churchgoer. I recall asking an usher in the huge church in Cirencester whether she knew of any Green Men in the building. She replied that they had no Green Men, but they did have a 'Tom and Jerry'. She then directed me to a delightful carving of a cat and a mouse in the Lady Chapel! Later I discovered that, to the mediaeval mind, a cat usually suggested evil and heresy, and that a carving of a cat in pursuit of a mouse or bird, or carrying one in its mouth, could be intended as a warning to unwary Christians not to allow themselves

A capital in the nave of the Basilique St Julien, Brioude, Haute Loire, Auvergne. Twelfth century. Photo: Ruth Wylie.

to be ensnared by heresy. A frog could also have sinister connotations and be associated with the Devil, because of the reference in the sixteenth chapter of the Book of Revelation to three unclean spirits 'like frogs', which came out of the mouths of the dragon, the beast and the false prophet. Misericords, being largely hidden from view, are less likely to be didactic than capitals and corbels, but even there amusing domestic scenes, or ones involving animals, often have a moralizing or allegorical meaning.

The mediaeval world was one in which almost anything and any subject could be conscripted into the service of the Church and used to enforce its teachings. The lewd and the lurid coexisted with terrifying monsters and the holy and just, and all with a single purpose in mind: to save sinners from temptation and Hell, and to bind them to the Church.

Nothing was considered as an unsuitable subject if it brought home the need to avoid sin and to be ready at all times to meet one's

Maker. Mediaeval carvers had no compunction even about portraying a pope dying suddenly, seated on the lavatory, and being carted off to Hell by three horned devils, because he had died unprepared and without time for repentance (Saint-Hilaire, Semur-en-Brionnais, Saône-et-Loire, France).

The former collegiate church of Saint-Pierre-de-la-Tour in Aulnay-de-Saintonge (Charente-Maritime, France) has a great assortment of images on the archivolts above the portal of its south transept. Here there are haloed Apostles and Prophets, crowned Elders of the Apocalypse, mermaids, an owl, a centaur, a donkey playing the harp, a bird with a man's face and a snake growing out of the top of its head like a crest, and a whole chain of foliate roundels containing heraldic animals and linked by spewing heads. On a pillar in the apse of the same church, there is a carving similar in style to the many Romanesque 'cat-faces' which disgorge foliage, except that, instead of a 'cat-face', there is a naked figure in the pose of an exhibitionist apparently defecating, or possibly giving birth to, stems and leaves!

The church of San Marin in Frómista (Spain), on the pilgrimage route, has several carvings representing all things sexual as emanating from the Devil, and suggesting an association between the vulva and the Mouth of Hell. On the northern side of the tower there is a naked monk, playing the lute and displaying his penis, while on the consoles of pediments there are two phallic men – one with a hugely enlarged penis, and the other in close proximity to a female exhibitionist.

A less crude anti-sex symbol was the mermaid, who in Romanesque church sculpture was yet another warning against debauchery. On a capital in the church of San Sigismondo in Rivolta d'Adda (Lombardy, Italy), dating from about 1100, there is a double-tailed mermaid. Her face is far from beautiful, and she is holding up her tails to either side in a provocative manner. Another double-tailed mermaid, on a fragment of carving preserved in La Cour d'Or, in Metz (Lorraine, France), is of particular interest to Green Man enthusiasts: her twin tails, also splayed to either side, turn into curling foliage above her head, and she is flanked by creatures with forelegs, long jaws and reptilian foliate tails, which are disgorging coiling stems with stylized leaves or flowers.

Not everyone in the Romanesque world shared the prevailing enthusiasm for grotesque monsters, ugly sinners and fantastic beasts. There were those who came to believe that they were counterproductive. All forms of lavish decoration in churches, especially monastic ones, were rejected by the Cistercian Order. This came into being in 1098 when a group of monks, who felt that the Benedictine Rule was not being followed sufficiently strictly, left the Cluniac Abbey at Molesmes and founded a new house at Cîteaux. Initially they encountered great hardships and immense difficulties. Their fortunes turned in 1112 when they were joined by Bernard of Clairvaux and some thirty companions, including his five brothers. Whereas Cluniac monks concentrated on making their abbeys centres of learning and art, with the result that towns grew up around them, the Cistercians devoted themselves to agricultural work and their abbeys remained isolated in rural settings.

St Bernard believed that elaborate architecture and sculpture were an unnecessary extravagance which distracted monks from their devotions: 'What profit is there in those ridiculous monsters, in that marvellous and deformed comeliness, that comely deformity? To what purpose are those unclean apes, those fierce lions, those monstrous centaurs, those half-men, those striped tigers, those fighting knights, those hunters winding their horns? Many bodies are there seen under one head, or again, many heads to a single body. Here a four-footed beast with a serpent's tail; there a fish with a beast's head... We are more tempted to read in the marble than in our service books and to spend the whole day in wondering at these things than in meditating the Law of God.' [trans. Coulton 1910: 72]

The Cistercian initiative found favour with many people, and, by the end of the thirteenth century, the Order had some seven hundred houses, all built to much the same pattern and characterized by their unadorned simplicity. Important Cistercian monasteries in Britain include Fountains Abbey, Tintern Abbey and Rievaulx. The presence of a wonderful Green Man (the one which inspired Kathleen Basford to undertake her pioneering research) above one of the windows of the Chapel of Nine Altars at Fountains Abbey, poses something of a problem. It is not Romanesque and clearly not part of the original building. According to Kathleen Basford, it was inserted during repair work done late in the fifteenth century. By then, the Cistercians may have become less strict in their views, like the Cluniac brethren before them.

Fountains Abbey is well worth a visit for its unusual Green Man (and much else), but, by the nature of their austere beauty, most Cistercian foundations have little or nothing in the way of foliate heads.

137

Above: *An initial 'M' from the Stuttgarter Passionale. Twelfth century. Copyright Bildarchiv Foto Marburg, LA 2211/1.*

Opposite: *The dedication page of the Codex Egberti. 980 AD. Copyright Bildarchiv Foto Marburg, neg. 59662.*

Where to look and what you will find

Heads – often reptilian and animal – abound in the elaborate patterns found in the metalwork of the ancient Celtic tribes, in the art of the Vikings, and in the manuscripts illuminated by Irish monks, but they do not seem to be directly related to the disgorging, full-face head typical of the Romanesque and later periods. Such heads begin to appear in manuscripts during the late tenth century, and somewhat later in stone carvings.

In some manuscripts, foliate heads occur in illuminated capital letters, especially the initial 'B' on the Beatus page of psalters. The Beatus page is so called because Psalm One begins with the words *Beatus vir qui non abiit* ('Blessed is the man who walketh not in the counsel of the ungodly... '). Often the fierce face of a lion or monster

can be seen, facing the downstroke of the letter 'B' at the join of the two curving sections.

Foliate heads may also form a decorative border, as they do on the dedication page of two late tenth-century books presented to Egbert, Archbishop of Trier from 977 to 993 and Imperial Chaplain and Chancellor of the Empire. Both books were created in the scriptorium of a monastery either in Trier itself or in Reichenau (an island in Lake Constance).

The first book is a psalter (now kept in the Museo Archeologico Nazionale, in Cividale del Friuli, near Udine in Italy) and the border around the portrait of Egbert contains eight heads – four at the corners and four halfway down each side – disgorging curls of foliage which are being gnawed by sundry unidentifiable creatures – some with legs and tails, and some more snakelike, but all in profile. Some of the disgorging heads are more human than animal.

The second book, known as the *Codex Egberti* (kept in the Stadtsbibliothek in Trier) is a book of *pericopes* or extracts. It was presented to the Archbishop by two monks of Reichenau, named Keraldus and Heribertus, who are drawn as tiny figures on either side of the Archbishop. The border differs in style from that of the psalter; there are only two full-face disgorging heads, one at the top and one at the bottom, and both are beastlike. Serpents are emerging from the ears of the upper head, and birdlike creatures from those of the lower one. More birdlike creatures are eating or disgorging each other along the sides, while the topmost ones are being swallowed by animals linked to the stems emitted by the upper head.

The combination of a full-face disgorging head with attendant creatures in profile also occurs on an ivory crucifix, twenty inches high, made for King Fernando (Ferdinand) and Queen Sancha of León (northern Spain) in about 1063. It is one of only three early mediaeval ivory altar crosses to have survived, and it is now kept in the Museo Arqueologico Nacional in Madrid. Its original place, however, was on the high altar of the collegiate church built in León on the orders of the royal pair to house the relics of St Isidore of Seville. León is on the pilgrimage route to Santiago de Compostela, and so the cross would have been seen by many pilgrims. The more influential of them may have been able to take a closer look at its magnificent carving. This, according to Peter Lasko, shows some influence of Ottonian art, and, in particular, of the crosses commissioned by Abbess Mathilde of Essen. [Lasko 1972: 150]

The front of the León cross has elaborately ornamented borders, with numerous deeply undercut figures of men and animals, crowded together and bent into all kinds of strange positions. Below Christ's feet, there is a larger figure of Adam. It is, however, the back of the cross which is of greater interest to us. This has the Lamb of God in the centre, and a symbol of one of the Four Evangelists at each extremity. The rest of the cross is decorated with *rinceaux* (circles of foliage) containing figures of men and beasts, including a centaur. The *rinceau* just above the Lamb contains a small, full-faced head disgorging stems, and, on either side of it, there are large, long-

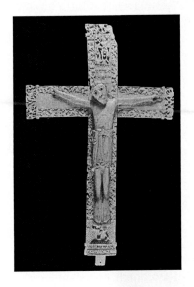

Top left: *Front of the ivory cross made for King Fernando and Queen Sancha of León. c.1063.*
Top right: *Reverse side, showing foliate heads above the Lamb of God. Copyright Archivo Fotográfico, Museo Arqueológico Nacional, Madrid.*
Bottom: *Detail of back showing Green Man.*

necked quadrupeds whose heads in profile, disgorge foliage. The main stem which forms this particular *rinceau* is decorated with small bead-like dots.

Several twelfth-century churches are decorated with sculptural compositions which include full-faced disgorging heads and others in profile. Among them is the former abbey church of Saint-Pierre in Moissac (Tarn et Garonne, France). This has an impressive Last Judgement in the tympanum over the south portal, dated 1120–35. At the bottom corner to Christ's left, there is a full-faced animal head, which disgorges two wide ribbons, decorated with dots. These ribbons go right round the upper periphery of the tympanum, with many folds and turns, and ultimately enter the mouth of a long-nosed beast shown in profile at the bottom corner to Christ's right. Similar long-nosed beasts, positioned at either end of the lintel below the tympanum, disgorge a row of *rinceaux* along the lintel.

A combination of full-faced and profile foliate heads can also be seen over the south portal of the abbey church of Saint-Pierre at Beaulieu-sur-Dordogne, not far from Cahors in France. The church dates from 1130–44. Here, however, foliate heads occur only on the lintel of the tympanum, and not all round it. The tympanum depicts the Second Coming of Christ, with angels sounding trumpets and the dead pushing up their coffin-lids to appear at the Last Judgement. At one end of the upper frieze on the lintel, there is a beast in profile disgorging ribbons which pile up at the other end, behind a fearsome full-faced head with a huge mouth that is either swallowing or disgorging some kind of animal. This animal, in turn, is doing the same with a man. In this particular context regurgitation is more likely than swallowing because in mediaeval times there existed a widely held belief that, prior to the Last Judgement, wild creatures would regurgitate the limbs or bodies of those whom they had eaten, so that their owners could be resurrected whole [Toman 1997: 329]. The lower frieze of the same lintel consists of rosette-like *rinceaux* with monsters of the kind that St Bernard condemned superimposed upon them, There is, for example, a creature with five heads in front and two more on its tail – a reference, perhaps to the seven-headed beast of the Apocalypse (Revelation 13.1).

The former convent church of St Cyriakus in Gernrode (Saxony-Anhalt, Germany) has a Holy Sepulchre (similar in purpose to the English Easter Sepulchre), dated between 1100 and 1130. On its outer wall a statue of Mary Magdalene stands between columns and surrounded by a frame composed of various animals and birds with symbolic Christian meanings, and the figures of Moses and John the

The Last Judgement in the tympanum over the south porch of the former abbey church of Saint Pierre, Moissac, c. 1115. Reproduced from Early Mediaeval Art *by John Beckwith, 1974 by kind permission of Thames and Hudson.*

Baptist. Around the whole, there runs a square frieze, reminiscent of the Egbert manuscripts in that it consists of full-face masks, with foliage coming out of their ears, disgorging long curling stems that flow into the mouths of animals in profile.

Ripoll itself, whose abbot may have initiated the transfer of manuscript motifs to church architecture, has a small head (beast-like and lacking a lower jaw) disgorging circles of stems and foliage down one of the jambs of the west portal of the abbey church of Santa Maria (second quarter, twelfth century) [illustration in Toman 1997: 295].

Not all churches have a tympanum with apocalyptic scenes over their main entrance. Some have portals decorated with a series of elaborately carved archivolts. Here, too, foliate heads can sometimes be found. Animal masks linking chains of *rinceaux* can be seen on the innermost of four archivolts, richly decorated with Biblical figures and animals both real and fabulous, above the south transept portal of the former collegiate church of Saint-Pierre-de-la-Tour in Aulnay-

143

de-Saintonge (Charente-Maritime, France), dating from some time after 1130 [illustration in Toman 1997: 270].

Above the west portal of the former abbey church of Sainte-Marie-des-Dames at Sainte (Charente-Maritime) a feline head disgorges *rinceaux* in a decorative frieze which separates the innermost archivolt from the second. The head is just above a medallion containing the Hand of God, held by two angels over the middle of the entrance, and just below the Lamb of God on the next major archivolt. The portal dates from between 1130 and 1160 [illustration in Toman 1997: 274].

The west façade of the former collegiate church of Notre-Dame-la-Grande in Poitiers (Vienne, France) is decorated with tiers of blind arches and niches containing statues of Biblical personages and scenes, including an unusual Tree of Jesse, which emerges from the latter's head in two branches, instead of from his loins. At least seven full-face disgorging heads can be seen among the foliage which adorns the columns and arches around the main figures. The façade was probably completed about the middle of the twelfth century.

Tympana with scenes from the Apocalypse are not commonly found in England, but a relatively simple one, dated c.1160, can be seen on the church of St John the Baptist, in Elkstone, Gloucestershire. It shows Christ in Majesty pointing to the Lamb of God and attended by the symbols of the Four Evangelists: an eagle, a winged lion, a winged ox, and an angel. The scene is bordered with foliage, some of which is being disgorged by a cat-like Green Man in the bottom right-hand corner from the point of view of the viewer. Another disgorging head can be seen in the semicircle of heads, many with beaks, that borders the upper curving edge of the tympanum.

The twelfth-century church of St Leonard at Linley, in Shropshire, has a modestly-sized tympanum containing simply a curious, barely human, naked figure, surrounded by foliage and spewing out more.

The most common type of Romanesque foliate head is the 'cat-face', which disgorges vegetation whose stems seem as important as its leaves, if not more so. Such heads can be seen on the capitals of Romanesque churches in many countries, and often the stems are 'beaded'. Cat-masks disgorging whirling 'beaded' stems appear on the capitals of piers in the crypt of Canterbury Cathedral. One jawless cat-face, disgorging stylized leaves with 'beaded' stems, has two wyverns rising above it in profile, looking backwards at each other. In St Anselm's Chapel, off the south aisle of the cathedral, there is

A capital in the ambulatory of the Basilique St Julien, Brioude,
Haute Loire, Auvergne. Twelfth century. Photo: Ruth Wylie.

another capital with masks disgorging 'beaded' stalks or ribbons. Deborah Kahn suggests that this is similar to a capital in the church of La Trinité in Caen, confirming the spread of fashions in motifs from one country to another [Kahn 1991]. French masons and Caen stone played an important part in the building of the cathedral, and Caen stone and 'cat-face' designs were also used for capitals in Reading Abbey.

In its day, Reading Abbey was an important monastic house, founded by Henry I, who personally laid the foundation stone in 1121. He was also buried before the high altar of the church. Monks from Cluny and its daughter house at Lewes formed the first community at Reading. Its principal relic was the hand of St James the Apostle, brought from Spain and presented to the Abbey by Henry I. This made the Abbey a centre of pilgrimage until the Abbey was dissolved in 1539 and demolished. Fortunately a few stones, including several capitals, were eventually recovered and are now displayed in Reading Museum. Some of these capitals are carved with feline-faced creatures disgorging 'beaded' stems. On one of them, the creature is flanked by two other beasts in profile.

The twelfth-century church of St Kyneburga at Castor, near Peterborough, has several Green Men on its capitals. One particularly fine 'cat-face' is disgorging foliage with long 'beaded' stems, which, unusually, it is holding with human hands. Another is breathing out foliage through its nose, while a third is simply spewing it out in a more conventional way.

Disgorging 'cat-faces' are not confined to tympana and capitals, but are found in other parts of churches. The mid-twelfth-century font in St Mary's Church, Stottesdon (Shropshire), for example, is decorated with a chain of roundels linked by 'cat-faces', while a lectern (c.1180) from Much Wenlock Priory, now preserved in the Victoria and Albert Museum, has small feline heads, upside-down and disgorging coils of stylized foliage on each of its three wider sides.

Disgorging lion-faces and heraldic animals and birds with foliated tails also appear on Russian churches dating from the twelfth and thirteenth centuries. Some of the motifs are so similar to those found in the West that direct influence must be supposed. Western architects and masons, as well as local ones, were sometimes employed by the Russian princes who commissioned the buildings. Heraldic beasts with foliate tails can be seen in large numbers on the exterior of the Cathedral of St Dmitri in Vladimir, built between 1194 and 1197 by Prince Vsevolod III [Faenson and Ivanov 1975: plates 56–60], while several heads, semi-human, semi-feline, disgorge foliage in its doorway [Anderson 1990: 18]. Typically Romanesque lion heads, lacking a bottom jaw and disgorging long stems, decorate the south facade of the Cathedral of St George in Yurev-Polsky [Faensen and Ivanov 1975: plates 72 and 79]. This was originally built between 1230 and 1234 by Prince Svyatoslav Vsevolodich, but, in the fifteenth century, it collapsed and was rebuilt. The restorers appeared unable to fit the sculpture together in the original sequence, so that it is now somewhat muddled in arrangement.

Curiously enough, 'cat-faces' reappear in the nineteenth century in some Bulgarian churches. In the central church of the Rila

*Detail of the font in the church of St Mary, Stottesdon, Shropshire.
Twelfth century. Photo: Ruth Wylie.*

Monastery there are at least two jawless 'cat-faces' disgorging foliage
on the iconostasis. Another disgorges flowers at the base of the
pulpit. Above this head several triangular panels, edged with strings
of 'beads' and decorated with oriental jugs containing bouquets of
flowers, spread upwards to the main part of the pulpit.

The Bulgarian wood-carvers may possibly have seen
Romanesque foliate heads in Russia, or closer to home in the Balkans
(at the Studenica Monastery, for example, built in neighbouring
Serbia as a royal mausoleum about 1200). Alternatively, the creatures
may represent the lion emblem of Bulgaria. The nineteenth century
was a period of intense struggles for cultural and political
independence, in which the Church played an important role. These
foliate heads are not, however, the only ones in the monastery
complex. In a small chapel, dedicated to St Luke and forming part of
a hermitage outside the monastery walls, there is a mural, dated
1790, in which leaf-masks form the main decoration on the golden
throne of a king.

Some Romanesque churches have recognizable non-feline
'green' animals. The old cathedral in Salamanca, Spain, for example,
has a bull disgorging foliage above the capital of one of the nave
pillars (mid-twelfth or early thirteenth century). Nearby is a winged
reptile, with fore-legs and a long tail.

A capital in the crypt of the Cathedral of St Bénigne, Dijon, Côte d'Or, Burgundy. Ninth century. Photo: Ruth Wylie.

A much older 'green' bull can be seen at the easternmost end of the Christian world – in Georgia, in the Caucasus. Christianity became the state religion of Georgia in the sixth century, but there had been bishops in the western part of the country since the fourth century. The 'green' bull's head, which has some damage to its horns, originally decorated a fifth-century basilica, but was later incorporated into the east façade of the eleventh-century church of Sveti-Tskhoveli, in Mtskheta, near Tbilisi [illustration in Mepisashvili and Tsintsadze 1979: 69].

The Green Men most typical of the Romanesque period have feline faces, but some are more human in appearance. An early example is the curious little person on a capital in the abbey church of Saint-Benigne in Dijon (Côte d'Or, France), who has his foliage bundled up and tied above his head, like the kerchief traditionally worn by sufferers from toothache! He dates from about 1000, when

The capital of the twelfth-century Hartmann column (so called because the mason left his signature upon it with a Latin sentence) from the former collegiate church of SS Simon and Jude in Goslar, Domvorhalle, Harz, Germany. The church once formed part of an imperial complex which included a palace built during the first half of the eleventh century. Photo: Ruth Wylie.

the church was commissioned by Abbot William of Volpiano, and is quite unlike any other known Green Men.

This also the case with most humanoid Romanesque Green Men, as opposed to 'cat-faces'. The latter appear to have been derived from a common source, while the former are far more individual. This is apparent in the examples to be seen in three German monastic foundations: the former convent church of St Servatius in Quedlinburg (Saxony-Anhalt), the former collegiate church of St Simon and St Jude in Goslar (Lower Saxony), and the former Premonstratensian monastery church of St John the Baptist in Spieskappel (Hesse).

Though otherwise quite different in appearance from each other, all three are bearded – which, in itself, is unusual – and, strictly speaking, only the last is truly 'green'. The Quedlinburg capital (before 1129) shows a human head whose moustaches turn into

The south doorway and tympanum of the church of SS Mary and David, Kilpeck, Herefordshire. Photo: Bob Trubshaw.

coiling winged creatures, with crocodile jaws that snatch at what might be foliage coming either from out of the sides of the head, or from behind it [illustration in Toman 1997: 315].

The Goslar capital (third quarter of the twelfth century) is thematically similar, but more sophisticated both in design and execution. The bearded human head is flanked by two winged reptiles, resembling wyverns and reminiscent of those in the cathedral in Salamanca. These reptiles link necks to form an arch above the head, and each places one fore-foot on the head's wavy hair, and the other near its mouth, from which the reptiles' coiled tails emerge, decorated with 'beads'.

The capital in Spieskappel (c.1200) is quite different again and particularly strange. It shows a large head with two stylized leaves emerging from its tightly closed mouth. Unusually it also has a body, small and hairy, and a long beard. To either side, at the corners of the capital, there are female heads wearing circlets over long tresses of hair that curl round to become the hairy arms of the Green Man, whose equally hairy legs are splayed out and coil over his arms to end in reptilian heads [illustration in Toman 1997: 315].

The tiny church of SS Mary and David in Kilpeck (Herefordshire) is of special interest to Green Man explorers, because its remarkable

Top: *The Green Man on a capital by the south doorway of the church of SS Mary and David, Kilpeck, Herefordshire.*

Bottom: *Detail of the voussoirs surrounding the tympanum over the south door of the church of SS Mary and David, Kilpeck, Herefordshire. Photos: Ruth Wylie.*

A capital in the nave of the Cathedral of St Lazare, Autun, Saône et Loire, Burgundy. Twelfth century. Photo: Ruth Wylie.

carving includes well-preserved examples of the main elements characteristic of Romanesque foliate heads. The church's founder, Oliver de Merlemont, made the pilgrimage to Santiago de Compostela and evidently examined and remembered what he had found in the monastic houses along the route.

Kilpeck has an archetypally unattractive 'Sheela-na-gig', who crudely and shamelessly displays on an outside corbel (see photo on page 133). It also has a definitive Green Man at the top of a jamb on the ornately carved main portal (1135–40). He is disgorging 'beaded' stems that end in foliage and an object resembling a fir-cone. On the opposite side of the doorway, rising above a sprig of foliage, there is a creature like a wingless wyvern, with a line of 'beading' running from its neck to the end of its long, twisting tail. Though not physically linked to the Green Man by stems, this creature strongly resembles the beast in profile that accompanies many Romanesque foliate heads.

Heads and 'fir-cones' on the west front of the church of Notre-Dame-la-Grande in Poitiers, Vienne, Poitou-Charente. Twelfth century. Photo: Ruth Wylie.

The tympanum contains, not an apocalyptic scene, but a single plant, possibly a Tree of Life. It, too, has 'beaded' stems, and there are also flowers of a kind found in other Romanesque sculptures and some of the mysterious 'fir-cones'. The two main archivolts around the tympanum also contain a number of Green Men: on the inner archivolt, two feline masks disgorge reptilian creatures, while on the outer archivolt, the carving consists of an animal-head at the base, disgorging nine medallions containing various birds, fishes, etc. and linked together in a chain by nine feline masks.

The motifs which, for the moment, we will call 'fir-cones' appear frequently in Romanesque sculpture. They are sometimes taken to be roughly carved bunches of grapes, although many of them point upwards or in other gravity-defying directions uncharacteristic of grapes. They also appear with leaves and flowers that certainly do not belong to vines – or to fir-trees, either.

Look carefully at Romanesque sculpture and you will sometimes find 'fir-cone' motifs associated with Green Men or with flowers that most closely resemble stylized lotuses – in which case the 'fir-cones' become lotus-buds.

One example can be seen on the facade of the church of Santa Maria in Pomposa (Emilia-Romagna, Italy), which dates from the second quarter of the eleventh century. Here the markedly oriental-style decoration consists of geometrically coiled stems, with cone-like buds, placed on either side of lotus-flowers, and framing small additional figures of men and beasts [illustration in Toman 1997: 300]. On a twelfth-century capital in Autun Cathedral (Saône-et-Loire, France), there is a peculiar naked figure, with legs but no arms, disgorging luxuriant foliage with 'beaded' stems and 'fir-cone' buds. 'Cones' are present in several of the Green Man examples already mentioned, including the frieze on the Holy Sepulchre in Gernrode, the west façade of Notre-Dame-la-Grande in Poitiers, and the 'Green Sheela' in St Michael's, Melbourne.

By concentrating their attention on the Green Men themselves to the exclusion of all else, many enthusiasts miss important clues that are staring them in the face. The plant in the tympanum at Kilpeck has something important to tell us. So has the 'wingless wyvern'! And so have the 'fir-cones'!

What this 'something' is will become clear after we have travelled and explored a little further.

7: PRE-ROMANESQUE
DISCOVERIES AND DEAD ENDS

We have reached a critical point in our journey of exploration. Up till now, each new step into the past has revealed yet more examples of foliate heads that seem to bring us ever closer to their ultimate source. Suddenly, however, the trail peters out. We need to stop and take stock of our surroundings.

Much of what was created in the centuries preceding the great Romanesque abbeys has either been destroyed or remodelled, but enough remains to give us a rough idea of the situation. Whether we examine grandiose imperial edifices, such as those at Ravenna and Agia Sophia in Istanbul, or modest vernacular buildings, such as our own Saxon churches, everywhere we encounter the same puzzling dearth of Green Men.

The foliate heads of the Dark Ages

The so-called Dark Ages are indeed dark when it comes to foliate heads. Few such heads have been recorded, and they are not particularly enlightening. We will, nevertheless, take a closer look.

In the Archeological Museum in Istanbul there are a number of capitals, dating from the sixth century AD and decorated with leaf-masks. On one capital, found in the city walls during excavations in 1972, cornucopiae appear between leaf-masks that clearly represent Okeanus, since they display his telltale crab's claws [illustration in Basford 1996: plate 6a]. Cornucopiae also appear between leaf-masks on capitals discovered in 1885 at Mudanya on the Asiatic shore of the Sea of Marmara, due south of Istanbul [illustration in Basford 1996: plate 7]. These leaf-masks are carved in a somewhat different style, using a more hollowed-out technique. The cornucopiae are brimming with grapes, and, although the curling upper leaves are reminiscent of crab's claws, there are, in fact, no visible claws. This prevents a definite identification with Okeanus, although the latter is sometimes portrayed without them.

Another capital in the Istanbul Museum is decorated with what appear to be actual masks, because the faces below the leaves are cut off just above the eyebrows [illustration in Basford 1997: plates 8a and 8b]. Various other capitals with leaf-masks of differing designs are also exhibited in the Museum, demonstrating the continued popularity of the motif in the Roman world.

The Rheinisches Landesmuseum in Trier houses a number of leaf-masks, dating from the second or third century AD, which shed some light on the history of the motif. Some of them are to be found on the sarcophagi of wine merchants which actually take the form of wine-ships and were discovered at Neumagen on the Mosel. Kathleen Basford was of the opinion that one of these leaf-masks almost certainly represents Okeanus, and thus symbolizes a safe journey to the Islands of the Blessed – a paradise for the righteous dead, believed to lie in the great River Ocean. The other leaf-masks in the same museum, including some entirely fashioned from leaves, are harder to interpret. Kathleen Basford admits the possibility that although they, too, might represent Okeanus, they might equally have Bacchic significance – something quite feasible in a major wine-growing area. Participants in Dionysian rites are known to have made themselves crowns of leaves, which could have extended into masks [Basford 1996: 9–10; plates 3a and 4a].

One foliate head which poses something of an unsolved riddle can be seen in the church of Saint-Hilaire-le-Grand in Poitiers. It is carved on the lid of the sarcophagus of St Abre and is thought to date from the fourth or fifth century.

St Abre was the daughter of St Hilaire, or Hilary, (c.315–c.367), who was Bishop of Poitiers and a learned theologian. He was sufficiently well-known in England for his name to be given to the 'Hilary Term' of universities and law courts, which begins on or around his feast-day of January 13. He was born into a wealthy, cultured pagan family and, having converted to Christianity, he became an implacable opponent of Arianism – a heresy which alleged that Christ was not coequal and coeternal with God the Father, because the Latter had created the Former. Arianism was rejected by the First Council of Nicaea (325), called by the first Christian Emperor, Constantine the Great, but it came close to triumphing when his successor, Constantius II, chose to support Arianism. In 356, Constantius banished Hilaire to Phrygia in Asia Minor, where the zealous Bishop made himself such a nuisance to the local Arians that they sent him back to Gaul in 360.

The carving on his daughter's sarcophagus shows a benign human face, like a sun, or a flower surrounded with petal or bracts. At first glance, it is reminiscent of the faces favoured by the builders of the Perpendicular portions of Gloucester Cathedral some thousand years later. However, while those in Gloucester do not disgorge anything, the Poitiers head fills the whole shallow arc of the lid with stems, foliage and large five-petalled flowers. Whether or not we can regard this head as a true 'disgorger' is debatable, because the vegetation emerges, not from its mouth, but from its nose, and, moreover, not even directly from its nostrils, but out of two cornucopiae connected to them.

The uniqueness and significance of the foliate head on St Abre's tomb are open to debate. There are other, later, instances of cornucopiae in association with foliate heads and of foliage emerging from the nostrils rather than the mouth. We have already noted the cornucopiae on Martin Luther's *Appeal* of 1520, and on the frame of Tintoretto's painting, as well as the foliate head breathing out leaves on the tomb of William Harrington (1350) in St Chad's Church, Harpswell, Lincolnshire. Although it has no cornucopia, the Green Man on a roof-boss (fifteenth century, restored in the seventeenth century and repaired in the late nineteenth century) in the church of St Peter and St Paul, Kettering, bears some resemblance to St Abre's Green Man in that it has 'petals' around its face and is exhaling through its nose.

If there is a common thread between all these surviving images, it is likely to lead us back to classical times. St Abre's tomb dates from a period when Christian iconography was barely established and still borrowed heavily from Roman models. It was still the custom to portray Christ himself beardless, like a youthful pagan god or Roman aristocrat, when the Ostrogoth King Theodoric (474–526), who was an Arian Christian, established his capital at Ravenna and erected a baptistry and the church of Sant' Apollinare Nuovo. His Arian baptistry contains a mosaic representation of Christ's baptism in which the River Jordan is shown personified as a Roman river god, with an urn and a head-dress of crab's claws.

Pagan deities and pagan survivals

The Green Man has so often been described as a pagan god, a forest spirit, or a fertility symbol that many people assume unquestioningly that this is so. But is it?

Exactly which pagan god or spirit is the Green Man supposed to represent? And why was he everywhere tolerated by the none-too-tolerant Church?

These were the key questions that we asked ourselves at the start of our journey of exploration. Now that we have arrived at the point at which the Green Man first appeared in Christian art, it is time to provide some answers.

So, who is the Green Man?

Okeanus is an obvious candidate as far as visual form is concerned. Both the leaf-mask and the Italianate Green Man can confidently be traced back to models representing the Titan. When we consider content, however, things are less straightforward. Even to the Romans, Okeanus was a superannuated minor deity, lacking shrines and temples. His image was more of an auspicious ornament than a genuine religious symbol. Despite his numerous mythical offspring, Okeanus was never seen as a fertility god. Neither was he in any way associated with forests. His marine nature is clearly visible in the great silver dish, dating from the fourth century AD, discovered at Mildenhall in Suffolk and now on view in the British Museum. Here Okeanus is portrayed with a beard of seaweed, out of which dolphins are peeping, and all around him are some of his daughter nymphs.

Another source of inspiration for foliate heads, especially the uglier kind, is the Medusa or Gorgon, whose decorative potential was grasped, time out of mind, by Pallas Athene herself. The goddess placed the severed head of the monster killed by Perseus on her own shield, and Gorgons' heads appear throughout the Greek and Roman world as motifs in sculpture, mosaics, paintings, and ornamentation on vases. Bath has a splendid Romano-Celtic example of what appears to be a male Gorgon, with moustaches, which originally formed part of the pediment of the Temple of Sulis Minerva. As well as snakes, the Bath Gorgon has tiny wings on each side of its head, a feature which also appears in an image of the Gorgon from Pompeii. Like Okeanus's seaweed, the Gorgon's wild mop of writhing snakes can readily be transformed into leaves, although Gorgons are in no way connected with either forests or fertility, and were never worshipped as gods.

At first sight, the only known inscription to put a name to the Green Man offers a more promising lead. The inscription consists of a single word 'Silvan' – in rather rough letters, inscribed above a foliate face on a fountain made about 1200 for the cloisters of the Abbey of Saint-Denis in France. The head, which has oak-like leaves sprouting from its brow, is one of several representing Roman deities carved between the spouts of the basin of the fountain. Silvanus was one of the many Roman gods associated with agriculture and fertility and often confused with each other, among them Faunus, whose image also appears on the fountain. As his name suggests, Silvanus was a forest god, who also watched over aboriculture and the work of clearing woods to make fields and pasture. His, too, was the

The end panel on the lid of the tomb of St Abre in the church of
St Hilaire-le-Grand, Poitiers, Vienne, Poitou-Charente, France.
Fourth century. Photo: Ruth Wylie.

protection of the herds that grazed on the pastures, and cattle would be sacrificed to him.

Before leaping to the conclusion that the Green Man is the sylvan pagan god, we need to remember that Silvanus never appeared in Roman iconography with a foliate face, although he might carry a tree and a pruning-hook. It is therefore possible that the face on the fountain represents a unique identification on the part of the carver or commissioner, who, unsure of Silvanus's appearance but acquainted with foliate heads, simply decided to portray him in this manner. This is the conclusion reached by Kathleen Basford, who makes the point that, since there is no other evidence to suggest that the Green Man was widely known as Silvanus during the Middle Ages, this particular artist was just exercising his imagination [Basford 1996: 16; plates 23a and 23b].

Dionysus (Bacchus), the classical god of wine, is often assumed to be an aspect of some universal Green Man. Classical images of the god, crowned with ivy and vine leaves, may well have inspired some Gothic and Renaissance foliate heads, but we find no trace of him in the earlier, Romanesque period. Unless, of course, we are prepared to identify 'cat-faces' with the panthers that draw his chariot - an idea too farfetched to be seriously considered!

We will have the same difficulty in finding an exact, or even approximate, match when we look at the gods of the Celtic tribes which inhabited much of pre-Christian Europe. With some exceptions, these gods were seldom represented in the form of images until Roman times, when they tended to become identified or paired with Roman gods having similar characteristics or spheres of influence. One example is Sulis, the local tutelary Celtic deity of the hot spring at Bath, who was equated with the Roman goddess Minerva. A bronze head of the composite goddess, Sulis Minerva, and several dedications invoking her aid, have been found in Bath.

Even major Celtic deities who were worshipped by several, or even all, Celtic tribes, were similarly paired with Roman deities. Cernunnus was associated with Mercury and was often portrayed in his company or holding the purses appropriate to the Roman God of Commerce, in addition to having his own traditional attributes, which included antlers, torcs and ram-horned snakes. Cernunnus, however, unlike most Celtic gods, had acquired, and was portrayed with, his own well-defined iconography as early as the fourth century BC, as witnessed by a somewhat primitive rock-carving in Val Camonica (northern Italy) [Green 1994: 87]. Possibly the finest surviving portrayal of Cernunnus is to be found on one of the panels of the Gundestrup Cauldron, discovered in a Danish bog but probably made in what is now Bulgaria, during the first century AD. Whether or not there is any connection with Cernunnus, his characteristic ram-horned snakes can still be seen in Bulgaria as a favourite ornament on carved shepherds' crooks.

Despite the Celts' fondness for heads, to which they appear to have attached particular significance, Cernunnus is usually portrayed full length. In one unusual relief, now in the Corinium Museum in Cirencester, his legs have become ram-horned snakes. Like most Celtic deities he has numerous spheres of power. He is a part-human, part-animal Lord of Animals, both wild and domestic; a provider of abundance in the form of food and money; and a god of fertility and rebirth.

Some authors cannot resist the temptation of identifying every horned head as that of Cernunnus. William Anderson, for example, quite arbitrarily refers to the two foliate heads on the south porch at Moissac as 'Cernunnus heads'. Both heads, however, have short, bull-like horns, whereas Cernunnus invariably has antlers. These link him to the deer, whose king or brother he appears to be, and possibly also to the forest trees, which branch like antlers. Even the largest and most impressive antlers are shed annually and renewed, and the enaction of this may have formed part of the rituals performed in his honour, since some figures of Cernunnus have removable antlers [Green 1994: 86].

Opposite: *Foliate heads on the jambs of the south portal of the former abbey church of St Pierre, Moissac, Tarn and Garonne, Midi-Pyrenees. Twelfth century. Photo: Tina Negus.*

A fifteenth-century misericord in the Cathedral of the Holy Trinity,
Norwich, Norfolk. Photo: Ruth Wylie. Reproduced by kind
permission of the Chapter of Norwich Cathedral.

None of the surviving images of Cernunnus has a foliate face,
but there is one Celtic god who is sometimes portrayed with a leaf-
crown. This is the Gaulish hammer-god, known as Sucellus and
associated in southern Gaul with the Roman god Silvanus. His leaf-
crown is, however, merely an occasional addition to his
iconography, and his constant attributes are his hammer and a pot.
Thus neither Cernunnus nor Sucellus seems a likely model for the
Green Man, whose greenery is not an optional extra but an integral
part of his image.

What may be leaf-crowns also appear on some much older
Celtic stone heads, found in southern Germany and uninfluenced by
Roman art. Dating from about the fifth or fourth century BC, these
heads have two great 'leaves' similar to a 'Tree of Life' or a Paisley-
pattern motif, ballooning up on either side of their faces. Some of
them (such as those on the stone pillar from Pfalzfeld, St Goar) have
three-pointed beards which might just be regarded as foliate, and a
trefoil on their foreheads [Cunliffe 1997: 126–7]. Trefoils occur on
the foreheads of a few Green Men in Britain, including one on a
misericord in Norwich Cathedral (fifteenth century); one on a
pendant in the retrochoir of Rosslyn Chapel, near Edinburgh (also
fifteenth century); one in All Saints' Church, Wilbarston,
Northamptonshire (thirteenth century); and one in the Church of
St Peter and St Paul, Kettering. There is, however, no evidence that
British craftsmen were aware of a few carvings created in Germany
over 1,500 years earlier. Coincidence of imagination is more
probable than any actual connection.

*A pendant boss in the east end of Rosslyn chapel, Roslin,
Midlothian. Fifteenth century. Photo: Ruth Wylie.*

The trail has become very faint indeed. Have you ever seen a
Green Man with antlers? Or a Roman, Greek, Celtic, or even
Egyptian, deity who disgorges foliage? No? In that case, we need to
do some serious re-thinking.

In order to get back onto the right track, we have to reject the
popular but anachronistic idea that the Green Man was smuggled
into churches by recalcitrant, underground pagans. There is no
evidence of any appreciable survival of paganism in Western Europe
at the time when the first known Green Men were created, let alone
of the presence of active, militant pagans in a position to influence
patrons, architects and masons in the numerous dioceses where
Green Men appear in monasteries and cathedrals.

Once Christianity had become the official religion of the Roman
Empire, it spread so rapidly and to such good effect that even the
barbarian invasions and the later Viking raids had little impact on the
Church's power. Those raiders who became permanent settlers soon
accepted the established faith. In most parts of western Europe, the

old religions had crumbled and vanished centuries before the first foliate heads made their appearance in Romanesque art and sculpture. The dissidents of the day were no longer the unconverted worshippers of Dionysus, Cernunnus and Woden, but convinced Christians who, for various reasons, found themselves at odds with the official Church and were, therefore, dubbed 'heretics'. A good general survey of 'pagan survivals' in Britain can be found in the last two chapters ('The Clash of Faiths' and 'Legacy of Shadows') of *The Pagan Religions of the Ancient British Isles* by Ronald Hutton [1991].

The Christian Church owed its rapid and complete victory over paganism in part to its skill in borrowing from the religions which it replaced such things as the dates of its major festivals and feast-days, and giving them a new, Christian content. Many deeply-rooted customs and superstitions received baptism and new clothes, so that they were perpetuated by devout Christians no longer conscious of their pagan origin.

The popular carol *The Holly and the Ivy* provides an excellent, if relatively modern, illustration of how something originally pagan – in this case, the age-old magical connection between evergreen foliage and the Winter Solstice – can be re-interpreted in Christian terms:

The Holly bears a blossom
As white as the lily flower,
And Mary bore sweet Jesus Christ
To be our sweet Saviour.
The Holly bears a berry
As red as any blood,
And Mary bore sweet Jesus Christ
To do poor sinners good...

Although the enigmatic lines about 'the rising of the Sun and the running of the deer' may sound like echoes of a time when people worshipped solar deities and the antlered Cernunnus, those who sing these lines sweetly in the choir at Christmas to 'the playing of the merry organ' are certainly not covert pagans, but good Christians.

The locations in which the earliest Green Men appear indicate clearly that they entered the Christian world with the blessing of the Church. Romanesque Green Men do not skulk in dark places under misericords or on barely visible roof-bosses. They are prominently placed for all to see on buildings designed for monks who had chosen holiness and renounced the world, and on costly items presented to godly persons holding high office in Church and State.

Whatever meanings they may once have had in a previous existence, they were brought into churches to serve the purposes of the Church. Of that there can be no doubt.

Given the innumerable examples of Green Men and their wide distribution, every Christian in western Europe must have been familiar with the motif. Yet, as we noted at the beginning of our journey, the dog did nothing in the night time: the motif raised no eyebrows and excited no criticism in the many mediaeval writings that touch on the subject of imagery in churches. Even St Bernard, who listed so many strange creatures to which he took exception, failed to mention anything that we can identify as a Green Man.

Everything that we have so far discovered points to the conclusion that foliate heads either played a neutral, decorative role, like acanthus leaves or dog-tooth, or else were recruited, like griffins and manticores, to press home some Christian teaching. The classical lineage of leaf-masks is obvious, but what about the disgorgers? What about the 'cat-faces'?

The Green Man and the Knights Templar

Some valiant attempts have been made to link the disgorging Romanesque 'cat-faces' with the Knights Templar, who were accused, among other blasphemous and shocking things, of worshipping a demon called Baphomet, who took the form of a head, a skull, or a cat. Such a link could exist only if the accusations against the Templars were true. We would then expect to find 'cat-faces' in all Templar churches and nowhere else. But not all Templar churches have 'cat-faces' and many non-Templar churches do. Moreover, the Order of the Poor Fellow-Soldiers of Jesus Christ and the Temple of Solomon – to give the Templars their full, official name – was founded in 1119, which is later than the earliest examples of 'cat-faced' Green Men. The most that we can assume is that, like other builders of mediaeval churches, the Templars played a part in popularizing and spreading an already existing motif.

If, however, the accusations against the Order were false, then the whole hypothesis is rendered null and void. Most historians have long suspected that the Templars were framed and persecuted between 1308 and 1314 to give Philip IV of France an excuse to appropriate their lands and treasure. Quite recently, such suspicions were confirmed by the discovery in the Vatican of a long-lost parchment showing that the Pope of the day, Clement V, became convinced of their innocence and decreed that they were absolved by the Church and could once again receive Christian sacraments.

[Owen 2002]. Unfortunately, Philip went ahead and put the leading Templars to death before the Pope's decree could be made public.

By clearing the Templars of all charges of heresy and other crimes, the papal document restores them to the status of a respectable, if rather dull, monastic order. To hope that we shall now hear no more of the absurd myths and theories that have been spun around their name is, perhaps, over-optimistic. In any case, even the myths offered no explanation as to why Baphomet should be disgorging foliage! No mention of leaves was made in the original charges made against the Templars! [Two excellent books about the Templars are Peter Partner, *The Knights Templar and their Myth* (1981), and Piers Paul Reid, *The Templars* (1999).]

A passing glance at the Anglo-Saxons

Modern seekers after mysteries and pagan survivals seldom pay much attention to the Anglo-Saxons. This seems unfair, since six of the eight Anglo-Saxon royal houses once claimed the pagan god Woden as their ultimate ancestor, and he, together with three other Anglo-Saxon deities survived the transition to Christianity enshrined in the names of the days of the week – Tuesday (Tiw's day), Wednesday (Woden's day), Thursday (Thor's day) and Friday (Frigg or Friga's day). Sadly, no certain images of Anglo-Saxon gods have survived, but there is no reason to suppose that any of them was portrayed as disgorging foliage.

It is, however, in early Anglo-Saxon Christian manuscripts (and not 'Celtic' ones) that we find disgorging feline faces, often as part of the elaborate decoration of the letter 'B' on the 'Beatus Page' of psalters made during the tenth and eleventh centuries. In one such example, the foliage flows from the mouth of a full-faced beast into those of subsidiary non-feline, animal profiles – a design similar in concept, if not in style, to the heads and foliage in the decorative borders of the books produced for Archbishop Egbert of Trier.

These manuscripts offer us some of the earliest known examples of disgorging heads as opposed to leaf-masks. The latter have Roman antecedents, but disgorging heads do not. Disgorging heads do not occur in the art of the early Celtic, Nordic or Germanic peoples either.

Where do disgorging heads come from?

Providing that we refuse to be sidetracked by the idea that the Green Man is an archetypal relic of some pagan belief once common to all

The Beatus Page from an Anglo-Saxon psalter of the early eleventh century. Here both the full-face feline head and two heads in profile can be seen. By permission of the British Library (Arundel 155 f.12).

the peoples on whose territory Romanesque and Gothic churches were built, we will be able to make some progress towards the answer.

To find the answer, we have to look further afield. There is one ancient image that combines all the features most characteristic of Romanesque foliate heads: a feline or monstrous full-face, flanked by non-feline faces in profile, all disgorging long, 'beaded' stems, and often flowers and 'fir-cones' as well.

The homeland of this image is India, where the full-face is called the kirttimukha and the profiles the makara.

8: THE INDIAN CONNECTION

Indian foliate heads have names that have conveniently remained unchanged for two thousand years and more. They also have legends, equally old, that explain every element in their iconography.

The kirttimukha and the makara

The kirttimukha is a face, fierce and suggestive of a lion or some kind of monster, with large bulging eyes and a wide mouth, often lacking a lower jaw, from which emerges what appears sometimes to be foliage, sometimes flowers, sometimes ribbons strung with beads, and sometimes curling foam or smoke.

The word kirttimukha means 'Face of Glory', and its origin is explained in several Hindu legends. One tells how an ambitious king, named Jalandhara, became so full of his own importance that he sent Rahu, the Eclipse Demon, to the God Shiva, demanding that he surrender his bride, Parvati. Shiva was so enraged that his anger burst forth from his third eye in the form of a lion-headed demon, which would have consumed Rahu, had not the latter cunningly taken refuge in Shiva, who was bound to protect him. Deprived of his victim, the newly created hungry demon begged Shiva to provide him with food. The god advised him to eat his own hands and feet - which he promptly did, and he continued eating until only his head remained.

Impressed by the creature's all-consuming power, Shiva declared that he should henceforth be known as kirttimukha, and that he should dwell by his door to protect the righteous and to deter evil-doers from entering. In Indian art and architecture, the kirttimukha often appears as an auspicious, protective symbol above doorways, and also above the mandorla or aureole, behind images of the gods.

According to another legend, it is Rahu's head which became the kirttimukha, and Vishnu who was the deity involved. In this story, Rahu manages to steal some *amrita* – the elixir of immortality made by churning the primaeval ocean. The Sun and the Moon report the theft to Vishnu, who takes a sword and beheads Rahu. Since the demon has already tasted the *amrita*, his head becomes immortal and wanders about the Universe seeking revenge on the Sun and Moon. Every time he catches up with either of these heavenly bodies, he swallows it, thus causing an eclipse, but each time it slips through his severed neck and escapes. This version of the legend not only provided a popular, easily understood explanation of eclipses, but also served to illustrate the futility of desire, which is an important teaching in Indian theology.

Neither of these legends, however, explains why the kirttimukha should disgorge greenery or beads. Indeed, this element of the image came from another mythical creature – the makara, which became associated with the kirttimukha during the Gupta period (fourth to sixth centuries AD). The makara combines the features of several creatures, including the crocodile, elephant, and fish or dolphin. Makaras are depicted as the *vahana* (mount or vehicle) of Varuna, God of the Waters. They also appear on the banners of Kama, God of Love and Fertility. While the kirttimukha first occurs in Indian art in about the second century AD, the makara was already in evidence during the third century BC.

The makara is found in both Hindu and Buddhist iconography. An early form of the creature can be seen on the red sandstone north gate-post of the Bharhut stupa (second century BC). Here a seductive *yakshi* (earth spirit) stands with her arm round a tree and her foot on the head of a makara [Craven 1987: 64–5]. Another fine example of a makara – this time clearly showing its elephant's trunk, crocodile's head and jaws, and fish-tail – appears on a carving which once stood at the doorway of an early fifth century temple at Beshnagar (north-east of Bhopal in Madhya Pradesh), and is now in the Museum of Fine Arts in Boston. Here a *yakshi*, probably representing the goddess Ganga, stands on the back of the makara to symbolize the sacred river.

The makara is also sometimes present in the famous image of Shiva Natarja – Lord of the Dance – immortalized in the Chola bronzes (tenth to twelfth centuries AD). In the course of his dance, Shiva creates, destroys and renews the cosmos, which is shown as a ring of flames encircling the deity and issuing from the mouths of two makara.

The makara was believed to disgorge wonderful things, among them the 'Cosmic Tree' or 'Wish-fulfilling Tree', usually depicted as a kind of vine or tendril derived from the sacred lotus plant, combined

Opposite: *Yakshi (possibly Ganga Devi). Indian, Gupta period, about 405-15 AD. Object place: Besnagar, Madhya Pradesh, Central India. Sandstone, 73.5 cm (28 15/16 in). Museum of Fine Arts, Boston. Charles Amos Cummings Bequest Fund; 26.26. Copyright 2002 Museum of Fine Arts, Boston.*

A kirttimukha and makara on a capital in Cave Number One at Ajanta, India. Late fifth century AD.
Copyright Benoy B. Behl.

with strings of pearls. When the kirttimukha and the makara are shown together these pearls may flow from the mouth of one into the mouth of the other. On a late fifth-century AD pillar in cave number one at Ajanta (north-east of Mumbai/Bombay), two makara flank a magnificent kirttimukha, with multiple strings of pearls joining their mouths.

In early Indian art, the lotus is often shown not merely as flowers and leaves, but also together with its root-like rhizome, which grows horizontally under water or mud [Singhal 1972 Vol.2: 56; illlustration 58]. The mysterious cone-like motif which we see in Romanesque sculpture is also in evidence, clearly identifiable as a lotus-bud. Examples can be seen in vases of lotus-flowers carved on the inner face of the north gate of the Great Stupa at Sanchi (first century BC to first century AD).

When the two images of the kirttimukha and the makara were combined, it was no longer obvious which was the disgorger and which the swallower. Since the combined image was used mainly as a protective device, the details of the myths surrounding its component parts were no longer of great importance. The differences between the two creatures became blurred, and the kirttimukha absorbed some of the attributes of the makara. As a result, even when

A detail of stone-carving on the north gateway of the Great Stupa at Sanchi. showing a vase containing lotus flowers and buds. The gateways and balustrades of the stupa were carved and dontated to the shrine by the ivory-workers' guild of Vidisha, a town near Sanchi. First century BC to first century AD. Copyright Helen Ward.

it appears alone, the kirttimukha now disgorges the pearls and lotus-stems of the absent makara.

Despite their Hindu origin, the kirttimukha and the makara were painlessly incorporated into the art of India's other religions – Jainism and Buddhism – in the role of auspicious, protective images. When Buddhism spread to neighbouring countries, including Tibet and China, the kirttimukha and the makara went with it, and their salient features were adapted to local needs.

A makara disgorging lotus flowers and a bud. From a medallion on the balustrade of the Bharhut stupa (1st century BC), now in the Museum of Calcutta. Copyright Helen Ward.

An exciting insight into what happened to the motifs in China was provided by items in an exhibition of sixth-century AD statues representing Buddhas and bodhisattvas at the Royal Academy in London during 2002. These statues had been unearthed by a bulldozer in the city of Qingzhou (Shandong Province, in north-east China) in 1996. One of the most beautiful exhibits was a free-standing bodhisattva, wearing elaborate jewellery, including two pendants adorned with disgorging animal masks. The more impressive of these masks disgorges strings of beads and pearly-petalled flowers.

Opposite: *A bronze Buddha from Tanjore (Thanjavur), South India, showing the traditional position of the kirttimukha and makara.*
Fifteenth or sixteenth century.
Copyright Victoria and Albert Picture Library.

Other items in the exhibition included fragments of triads – Buddhas, flanked by two smaller bodhisattvas and surrounded by a mandorla. In some cases, the bodhisattvas were sitting or standing on pedestals arising from lotus plants (sometimes complete with 'fir-cone' buds!), disgorged by dragons, which, on Chinese soil, replace the makara. The change is not as dramatic as it might at first seem, because the Chinese dragon, unlike its western relatives, is a benign, non-inflammable beast, traditionally associated with water and pearls, just like the original makara.

The Dorling-Kindersley Eyewitness book on *Religion* (1996: 28) has a picture of a beautiful oval amulet, showing a Tibetan adaptation of the kirttimukha in a mosaic of what appear to be turquoises, pearls, and other precious and semiprecious stones, set in gold. The fierce face, with tusks, pearly teeth and protruding ruby eyes, is intended to terrify hostile demons and to protect the wearer. Although there is no makara, the kirttimukha is disgorging golden stems bearing what seem to be lotus-flowers with petals made of pearls.

Parallels between Indian and Romanesque art

We are not the first to explore Indian territory in search of the Green Man. Others have been here before us. In most cases, however, their discoveries have either not been followed up, or failed to reach a wide enough public.

One of the very first to perceive a connection between Indian and Romanesque art was the French architect, E. Viollet-le-Duc, best known for his restoration of the mediaeval city of Carcassonne. In his *Dictionnaire Raisonné de l'Architecture Française du XIe au XVIe Siècle* (Paris, 1875, Vol. 7, 187 ff) Viollet-le-Duc suggested that the kirttimukha occurred on the facade of Notre Dame-la-Grande in Poitiers (c.1130–45). In 1931, an Indian scholar, Ananda K. Coomaraswamy, expressed his conviction that the makara occurred frequently in mediaeval European art [Coomaraswamy 1931].

These pointers inspired an American scholar, Millard B. Rogers (then Associate Director of the Seattle Art Museum, Washington State), to travel to Europe in the spring of 1959 in order to journey along the pilgrim routes to and from Santiago de Compostela, examining early Romanesque churches for signs of Indian influence. He found more than he had expected, and concluded that Coomaraswamy was correct and that Viollet-le-Duc's observation was 'an understatement'.

Standing Bodhisattva. Northern Qi dynasty (550–77). Qingzhou Municipal Museum, Shandong Province, China.
Copyright and reproduced by kind permission of the State Administration of Cultural Heritage, People's Republic of China.

Left: *Detail of the left side of the doorway at Kilpeck (shown complete in the photograph on page 150) with a makara-like motif. Photo: Bob Trubshaw.*
Right: *The kirttimukha-like Green Man on the opposite side of the Kilpeck doorway. Photo: Ruth Wylie.*

Rogers published an article about his findings in a leading American learned journal [Rogers 1960: 1176–82] but unfortunately this extremely important piece of research has largely gone unnoticed by those whom it would interest most – Green Man enthusiasts.

Rogers found that makara and kirttimukha appear on the majority of French and Spanish churches built during the twelfth century, but not on earlier Romanesque churches. He also noted that the use of the two motifs was discontinued after 1200.

His findings open up new avenues for exploration just when the trail is fading. Even if we know little about Indian art and have never visited the country, books and museums can equip us to look at Romanesque sculpture with new eyes.

We must not expect to see all the elements associated with the kirttimukha and makara in every Romanesque church. Variations and omissions also occur in Indian carvings, and we have to allow for the accidental changes that accompany repeated copying. Most Romanesque churches have little more to offer than the odd leonine kirttimukha disgorging tangles of long stems. There may not be anything resembling a makara, or it may take an unusual form. Even a solitary foliate head, however, may embody typical Indian features, such as the missing lower jaw of the kirttimukha, or the pearly stems, lotus-flowers or cone-like buds associated with the makara. Regardless of the range of elements present, the stylistic similarities between Indian and early Romanesque motifs are too close to be coincidental.

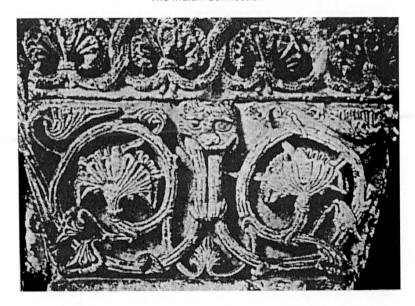

Fragment from the cloister of Saint-Etienne, Toulouse, c.1120, now in the Musée des Augustins, Toulouse. Note the lotus-like flowers. Reprinted with permission from Science, *Vol. 131, 1960. Copyright 1960 the American Association for the Advancement of Science.*

At Moissac, for example, the whole arc of the tympanum of the south porch is bordered by a ribbon ornament, studded with 'pearls', which runs from the mouth of a makara into that of a lion-faced kirttimukha (see page 143). The ornamentation on the lintel below consists of roundels of foliage issuing out of the mouth of two makara, with typically elephantine snouts, facing each other.

Rogers does not mention Kilpeck in his article, and almost certainly he never went there. Had he done so, he would surely have been delighted. Viewed in the light of the Indian connection, Kilpeck gains in excitement and importance. The disgorging Green Man on one side of the doorway is revealed as a kirttimukha, complete with pearly lotus-stems and a bud. The two-legged, long-tailed beast on the other side of the doorway then becomes a makara. The flowers and buds on the plant in the tympanum prove remarkably similar in style to those at the Great Stupa at Sanchi. And that is only the beginning! There is much more to intrigue and set us guessing.

Could, for example, the two beaded serpents issuing from the mouth of one of the heads on the tympanum arch be makara? And is

179

Above: *The kirtimukh and makara decorating a tympanum on the chapter house at Wenlock Priory, near Much Wenlock, Shropshire. Photograph by Mercia MacDermott.*

Opposite above: *A detail of the lintel (shown complete in the photo on page 143) of the twelfth century south portal of the former abbey church of St Pierre, Moissac, Tarn and Garonne, Midi-Pyrenees, showing a 'makara' below another profile head in the corner of the typanum.* Below: *A detail of the same lintel showing a 'makara' below the Green Man in the typanum. Twelfth century. Photographs and copyright: Tina Negus*

that another makara, with double, criss-crossing stems or ribbons, at the base of the arch, just above the Green Man? Have a good look (see pages 150, 151 and 178) and decide for yourself.

A carving even closer in style to the Indian kirttimukha and makara can be seen in the ruins of Wenlock Priory, which dates from the eleventh century. Here two long-snouted creatures, depicted in profile, both flank and are connected to a central feline head. The similarity to Indian examples is too marked to be explained away as mere coincidence.

As Rogers correctly observed, things changed after 1200. The Romanesque makara was forgotten entirely or transformed into a wyvern or some other creature. The kirttimukha, on the other hand, was imaginatively 'modernized' by Gothic sculptors, who perceived disgorged foliage as its only attribute, and substituted leaves of their own choice for the long-stemmed lotus-plants, which they neither recognized nor understood.

How Indian motifs reached the West

Establishing how Indian motifs reached the West offers a real challenge to Green Man explorers. The possible routes are unexpectedly numerous, but not well charted.

Distant as India appears to be from western Europe, trade and other contacts had united the two areas from classical times. About 45 AD, people came to understand the workings of the monsoons across the Indian Ocean, namely that in winter the prevailing winds blew from the north-east and in summer from the south-west. Using this knowledge, merchants were able to speed up maritime trade with India by bringing cargoes at the appropriate time to Egypt for distribution to the Mediterranean area. Here there was a tremendous demand among the richer citizens of the Roman Empire for costly oriental luxuries, such as pearls, gemstones, spices, ivory, perfumes, muslin and Chinese silk. Evidence of a Roman market for Indian *objets d'art* was provided by the discovery of an ivory figure of the Hindu goddess, Lakshmi, during excavations in Pompeii.

Indian embassies visited Rome during the early centuries AD, and there were Indian sects in Egypt during the Ptolemaic period. Indeed, the development of monasticism among the native Coptic Christians may have been the result of Asian influence from India, since neither celibacy nor meditation formed part of the older religious traditions of Egypt [Singhal 1972 Vol.1: 88; 103].

According to legend, St Thomas is supposed to have taken Christianity to southern India, but, even if he did not get so far, India was visited by Christian missionaries during the third century, when Pantaenus found an existing Church (rightly or wrongly said to have been founded by St Bartholemew).

As the first millennium AD progressed, India came to play a far more important role in western Europe than simply that of a provider of luxuries for the wealthy. The decline of the Roman Empire during the fourth and fifth centuries coincided with the rise of the Gupta Empire in India, which ushered in a golden age of art, literature and learning. For the first time, Hindu temples were built of stone, and it was at this time that the kirttimukha and makara were combined as a decorative element. The study of astronomy, medicine and mathematics flourished, preserving the learning of the ancient Greeks and making fresh advances. In mathematics, especially, India led the world, with the invention of the decimal system and the concept of zero. India's superior learning was gradually transmitted to a Europe

Lord Ganesha, protected by a kirttimukha and makara,
in the Hindu temple in Singapore.

still retarded in the Dark Ages through the Arabs, who were the leading traders and navigators of the time. Arabic manuscripts became treasured possessions in monastery libraries.

More direct contact between East and West, not always under the most favourable of circumstances, occurred in Spain after the Moorish invasion (711), and in Palestine, where the Crusaders captured Jerusalem in 1099. Both points of contact are worth exploring. The victorious Moors established centres of Arabic culture and learning in Córdoba, Granada, Seville, and Toledo, and their influence extended almost to the very walls of Santiago de Compostela. Raymond IV, Count of Toulouse and one of the leaders of the First Crusade (1096–99), held lands to the north of the Pyrenees through which most of the pilgrims passed and where examples of kirttimukha and makara can be seen in the abbeys where they rested and found shelter.

Rogers claims to have seen motifs derived from the legend of Rahu over the Islamic gateway in Aleppo, and in a section of the Talisman Gate in Baghdad. He concludes, however, that these Islamic carvings bear less resemblance to the original Indian models than the Romanesque foliate heads do, and that the motif must have reached Europe by another route.

One possible route is through the import of ivory carvings, together with unworked ivory for the use of European craftsmen. Another is through the import of Arabic manuscripts for royal and monastic libraries.

Here attention to dates becomes of the utmost importance. The earliest known Western disgorging foliate heads appear on manuscripts and artefacts, such as the León Cross, which predate the Crusades. The presence of foliate heads in Crusader churches may have helped to popularize the motif among Crusaders and pilgrims, but it could not have provided the original stimulus. Prior to the Crusades, there were Christian communities in Jerusalem that, despite Muslim rule, were able to worship freely. Unfortunately, we have no information as to whether there were any foliate heads in these early churches.

Manuscripts appear to offer the most promising leads. We already know of foliate heads on Anglo-Saxon manuscripts and on books prepared for the Archbishop of Trier at the end of the tenth century. According to Rogers, kirttimukha appear in Beatus manuscripts of Spanish origin (see page 130), one of the earliest known copies of which, made about 900, is now in the Morgan Library in New York. Illuminated manuscripts were an important

Two examples of Triple Hares in English churches.
Left: *A roof boss in South Tawton church, Devon.*
Right: *A floor tile from Chester Cathedral c.1300.*
Drawings by David Taylor.

source of guidance for masons engaged in pioneering work on the early mediaeval churches.

We can easily imagine an abbot embarking on the construction of one of the huge new monastic churches and discussing plans with his chief mason: 'And, over the main portal, make us a truly impressive Last Judgement, like this one'. He would then produce one of the treasured manuscripts from the monastery's library, perhaps, one of the many copies of the Beatus commentaries on the Apocalypse, with some eighty illustrations of the episodes described. The mason would examine it carefully, noting the iconography of the main figures and their arrangement. He might also be attracted by the less important elements, such as illuminated capital letters and decorative borders. Seeing a foliate head, he might decide to incorporate one into the border of his tympanum, together with the rosettes and coils of foliage which he had noticed on an ivory cross or reliquary.

Triple hares
The possibility that Green Men arrived in the West as migrants from the East is strengthened by the analogous case of the Triple Hares. This motif consists of three hares, or rabbits, running in an everlasting circle, with their paws on the circumference and their ears forming a triangle in the centre. At first sight each hare appears to have the requisite two ears, but a closer examination will reveal that the three animals have only three ears between them, and that each hare

shares an ear with its neighbour, in much the same manner in which the six Green Men on the roof boss in Chichester Cathedral share an eye (see photograph on page 92).

The Triple Hare motif is widespread in mediaeval churches both in England and continental Europe. It can, for example, be seen on roof bosses in several churches in the Dartmoor area of Devon, including Chagford, Cheriton Bishop, North Bovey, Sampford Courtenay, South Tawton, Spreyton, Tavistock and Widecombe. All these date from the fifteenth century. Other examples include a floor tile in Chester Cathedral (c.1300), a misericord in Beverley Minster and a stained glass window in Long Melford, Suffolk. In many churches in France, Germany and Switzerland the Triple Hare motif appears on roof bosses, and also as decoration on a thirteenth-century abbey bell. In Lyons Cathedral (France) the motif occurs in a four-hare variant, with the four shared ears forming a central square.

The Buddhist connection
Patterns composed of either three or four animals can be seen far to the East in Budhist paintings in the Ladakh region of Kashmir. The numbers three and four are both of special significance to Buddhists and, in Ladakh, hares are sometimes replaced by antlered deer – a reference to Buddha's first sermon in the deer-park at Sarnath.

The earliest known examples of the Triple Hare motif occur in Buddhist cave paintings dating from the late sixth or early seventh century in Dunhuang on the edge of the Gobi Desert in western China. Remote as Dunjuang may seem to us, it was once an important garrison town on the Silk Road, along which the motif appears to have travelled westwards, possibly in the form of designs on luxury textiles. At the Silk Road Exhibition organized by the British Library in 2004, the Three Hares could also be seen on Islamic Mongolian coins dating from 1281–2. Trier Cathedral in Germany boasts a silver reliquary of a slightly later date (late thirteenth or early fourteenth century) with the Triple Hare motif on its base. This casket is believed by some art experts to have originally been fashioned in southern Russia by Iranian craftsmen working for a Mongol client!

The Three Hares motif is beginning to attract its own following of 'spotters' and would-be interpreters. Numerous theories about its significance are already being put forward. Some even attempt to establish a link with the foliate heads which often occur in the same churches. Sadly, most of these theories are pure speculation with no real evidence to support them. Whatever meaning the motif may have had in its eastern homeland, or subsequently acquired in the

One of the earliest known depictions of Triple Hares, painted on the roof of a Buddhist cave shrine, Dunhuang, China (AD 589–618). Drawing by David Taylor.

West, it appears to have reached us purely as a decorative image, like so many other motifs before and since.

Triple Hares and Green Men

For Green Man explorers, however, the Three Hares have an importance that goes beyond their mere decorative value, in that their progress from East to West, from one religion to another, can to a certain extent be traced.

If a motif based on hares can thus migrate across the world, finding favour with Buddhists, Muslims and Christians alike, why should not the Green Man have made a comparable Odyssey?

The probability is that the disgorging Green Man originated in India. All the elements associated with the earliest Romanesque foliate heads are attributes of the kirttimukha or the makara, and cannot be found in any western European prototype. The possibility of Indian influence reaching the areas where Romanesque art developed is also abundantly present. The motifs could have travelled in many ways, along a variety of channels. We have yet to determine beyond doubt exactly how this happened. The secret may be concealed under our very noses in some museum, library, or ancient monument, waiting to be discovered by a persistent explorer following the right trail and looking in the right place.

The Viking connection

The activities of the Vikings are worthwhile investigating since, at the very time when disgorging heads first appeared in Western art, the routes followed by these intrepid seafarers stretched from Iceland

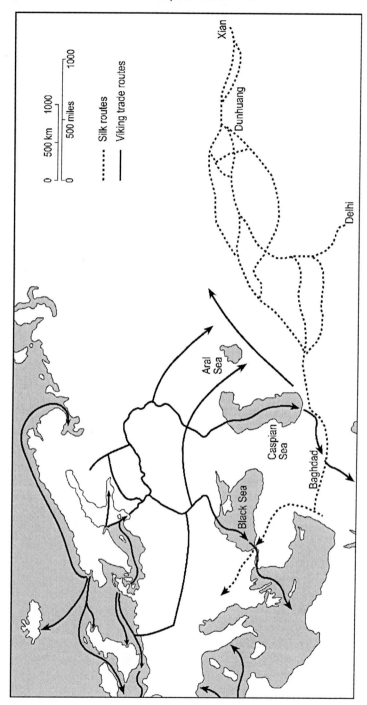

Viking trade routes and the routes of the Silk Road. Map by Anne Tarver.

Foliage-spewing animals on a twelfth-century font from Sweden, now in the Victoria and Albert Museum. Drawing by David Taylor.

to the Middle East and central Asia. The abiding popular image of Vikings as bloodthirsty pirates, who sacked monasteries and vented their fury on all who stood in their way, is only part of the picture.

The Vikings were traders as well as raiders. They sailed their elegant, superbly designed ships through the Bay of Biscay and past Gibraltar into the Mediterranean, and they followed the great Russian rivers down from the Baltic into the Black and Caspian Seas. From there, some would journey on even further on 'ships of the desert' overland to such centres of culture and international commerce as Baghdad and Khorezm, near the Aral Sea on the road to Samarkand. In Byzantium they appeared not only as merchants, but also in a different guise, as the elite Varangian Guard, which protected the person of the Emperor himself.

In their own environment, Viking craftsmen were as skilled and artistic as any in Europe, and fashioned beautiful objects out of metal, wood and stone. The Green Man enthusiast who starts examining their intricate, imaginative designs may well become hooked on the search, hoping every moment to stumble upon a familiar image, since Viking artefacts are crawling with coiling stems, stylized animals and enigmatic human faces. Some animals are even slightly foliate, such as the creatures on the panels of a twelfth-century Swedish font in the Victoria and Albert Museum, which appear to

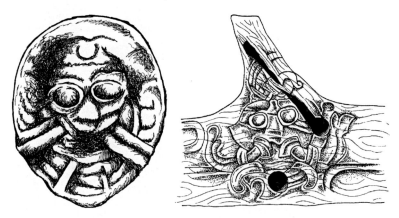

Two eighth-century Norwegian disgorging faces.
Left: *From sleigh shaft, Borre.*
Right: *Rowlock from a Gokstad boat.*
Drawings by David Taylor.

hold sprigs of leaves in their mouths, but which are not sufficiently early to have much bearing on our search for origins. On closer examination most Viking motifs turn out to be disappointingly not quite what we were looking for.

Of greater interest are two full-faced heads which can be seen on artefacts found in Norwegian ninth-century ship burials. Both seem to be disgorging, although only one could be considered even remotely foliate. The first is on a wooden sleigh shaft recovered from a burial at Borre, in the same region where the more famous Gokstad and Oseberg ship-burials were found. The second appears on a rowlock from one of the small boats belonging to the Gokstad ship.

Moreover, among the richer contents of the Oseberg ship there are items which hint tantalizingly at oriental connections. There is, for example, a wooden pail, known as the 'Buddha bucket' because its brass handle is ornamented with a cross-legged figure reminiscent of a Buddha. Its body is decorated with swastikas, which also abound as a motif woven into the tapestry and other textiles found in the burial. The swastika is an ancient auspicious symbol in India and the Far East, and also among native Americans. In the West, prior to Hitler, it appeared mainly in Roman mosaics, but I have also noticed swastikas on a badly damaged Greek statue of a woman, dating back to 500 BC, in the museum at Paestum.

If, as yet, no one has spotted any undeniable Green Man prototypes in Viking art, it may be that there are none to spot. On the other hand it may be that no one has looked sufficiently thoroughly. But even if the Vikings did not make any significant use of the motif, they could still have played a role in introducing it to the West in the form of merchandise from the East. Although the notion of Vikings riding camels may seem incongruous, ride camels they did, and we could certainly do with a peep into their saddlebags!

All this goes to underline the need for Green Man explorers to keep an open mind, and to be alert to the possibility for finding clues in some seemingly unlikely places.

9: UNDERSTANDING GREEN MEN

Our explorations, however incomplete, show a picture of the Green Man that differs radically from some commonly held current views of him. We have found no grounds for supposing that the Green Man is a once popular pagan deity who, refusing to fade away, was willy-nilly admitted to churches, or that he represents the underlying idea behind a multitude of folk customs and beliefs.

Ours is a more complex and exciting picture, which offers new challenges and opens new doors.

Foliate heads and folklore

The earliest examples of post-Classical foliate heads are to be found on manuscripts and artefacts made for the Christian elite and in churches built by the wealthy privileged classes, primarily for the use of monastic communities. The relationship between the Green Man and the less affluent, ordinary people, who formed the majority of the population, is obscure.

Attempts to link the foliate head to various aspects of the traditional culture of these ordinary people, such as folk customs, legends, songs, etc., seldom stand up to serious investigation, since such attempts tend to assume the existence of something akin to a 'Great Green Universal Principle' behind various phenomena which may appear superficially similar, but are disparate in origin.

Leaves, trees and flowers feature in numerous customs and rituals, but this does not automatically denote some connection with foliate images found in churches. Those who see the Green Man as the whole behind the parts, rather than a tiny part of the whole – the whole being the versatile use by all cultures of vegetation in imagery and symbolism – run the risk of reaching lopsided and erroneous conclusions. So far, no one has suggested that the crowning of a victor or poet with bay and laurel leaves once signified his symbolic transformation into the Green Man, or that a bride's wreath and bouquet once signified her mystic union with the Green Man! Yet some equally picturesque, but groundless, assertions have been made, and continue to be represented as fact.

Were the Green Man in any way connected with certain folk customs, these would have included some form of recognition of the carved images on or in the local church, such as the bringing of a wreath, the lighting of a candle, or a passing bow or muttered formula. There would be mention of the practice somewhere in surviving letters, memoirs, reports, parish records, or even court proceedings against blasphemers, idolaters and witches. So far, nothing of the kind has come to light.

Examination of such records does, however, reveal that many customs, or parts of customs, thought to be ancient are, in fact, of relatively recent origin. In Britain, this is partly the result of the suppression of many mediaeval traditions by the Puritans, and their later revival in a somewhat different form, often by enthusiastic, well-meaning intellectuals, dancing-masters and impresarios, and partly due to the fact that customs naturally evolve and change. Maypoles, for example, were known in mediaeval England, the earliest known references being from the fourteenth century. Banned by the Puritans in the 1640s, they returned to popularity after the Restoration, but the 'traditional' ribbons and plaiting dance were introduced only during the nineteenth century. In order to realize the need for caution in interpreting customs and their origins, we need only consider how, within less than a lifetime, the celebration of Hallowe'en has changed from remembrance of the dead, soul-cakes, apple-bobbing, divination and turnip lanterns to witches, bats, creepy-crawlies, and 'Trick or Treat'.

The foliate head of ecclesiastical architecture is not native to these Isles, but was brought here by Norman masons from the Continent. It owed its rapid spread, both in this country and throughout Europe, to the Catholic Church, monastic orders and pilgrims. Yet the motif never became so identified with Catholic dogma and ritual that it was unacceptable to Anglicans, Presbyterians, Lutherans and other Protestants. Even the most rigid Puritans evidently did not connect foliate heads with either popery or paganism, or else they would have attacked them as energetically as they attacked maypoles and statues of the Virgin. By then, foliate heads clearly had no particular hard and fast significance.

But was this always so?

A look at symbols and their uses

As we have discovered, foliate heads do not originate from a single source. Some types were present in Europe in Roman times; others came from further afield. All were probably adopted into Christian art by people who had little or no understanding of their original significance and who simply seized upon them as a novel, attractive alternative to straightforward acanthus leaves and other forms of ornamentation. From time immemorial in many parts of the world people have delighted in putting faces on such things as jars and images of the Sun and Moon. So why not enliven foliage as well?

Once they had been discovered and established in churches, foliate heads may well have been used, like animals from the bestiaries, to reinforce Christian teachings. They may have been used to illustrate the assertion, found in St Isidore's *Etymologies,* that evil men whose souls were already forfeit to the Devil were made to eat magic plants that transformed them into animals or hybrid creatures, or the fairly widespread belief that the Devil used coiled foliage to ensnare humans and bind them fast.

Any particular meaning given to foliate heads may not necessarily have remained constant or been everywhere the same. Like messages passed on by word of mouth, motifs imperfectly understood are liable to undergo strange changes as they travel. The recycling and re-interpretation of existing symbols to meet new needs and situations is nothing novel, but is a process which has gone on throughout history. Innumerable examples, both ancient and recent, can be cited to demonstrate how symbols can acquire different, even totally contradictory, meanings when transferred or borrowed.

Most people today would be surprised to learn that, in Britain, the robin redbreast was once widely regarded as a bird of ill-omen, especially if it appeared at a window, or entered the home. Even in the twentieth century, cases were recorded of people expressing alarm on the receipt of Christmas cards featuring jolly robins!

In China, chrysanthemums have for centuries been an auspicious symbol of long life and scholarship; in Japan, they form the traditional foundation of the Imperial Throne, but in modern Italy they have become so associated with funerals that they are never presented to people on other occasions. Some language textbooks even warn visitors to Italy never to take chrysanthemums to their hostess when invited to dinner!

During the twentieth century, the red field poppy, once associated with the Greek Corn Goddess, Demeter, acquired two special meanings that it never previously possessed. In Britain, it

Opposite: A twentieth-century Green Man in the garden of St Edmund Hall, Oxford. Sculpted by the Rev Graham Midgely. Photo: Mercia MacDermott. Reproduced by kind permission of the Principal of St Edmund Hall, Oxford.

became the symbol of Remembrance of those killed in battle. In Bulgaria, it became an emblem of the Communist Party.

Snakes are among the most ambiguous of symbols, revered and worshipped in many cultures, but demonized in Christian iconography. Olympias, mother of Alexander the Great, is said to have kept tame snakes as part of some ancient Balkan cult, and something of this tradition appears to have been communicated to later settlers in the area. More than eleven centuries of Christianity failed to dim the Bulgarian peasant's perception of the snake as the guardian of the home and the fields, or to deter his womenfolk from decorating ritual loaves baked for Christmas, Easter and other festivals with serpents fashioned out of dough.

The swastika is another now ambiguous symbol which Bulgarian peasant women might place upon their ritual loaves, or incorporate into their embroidery. Those who are aware of this ancient symbol only in its modern role as the emblem of Hitler's Nazis are often both shocked and surprised to encounter it in other far more ancient contexts – as an auspicious symbol in India (as early as the second millennium BC) and in Native American art; on a mosaic pavement at Lullington Roman Villa in Kent; or as decoration on the garments of a fragment of statuary, dating from the sixth century BC, found in the classical Greek colony of Paestum (Italy), to give just a few examples.

A curious feature of popular symbolism is that sometimes an evil thing can be transformed into a protective one. In the Indian myth, Shiva placed a demon's rapacious head on his doorway to deter other demons. In some parts of Bulgaria, the motifs embroidered on men's shirts included stylized representations of pests, such as caterpillars and snails, because it was formerly believed that this would prevent the real creatures from attacking the wearer's crops. Such reasoning was just one manifestation of a common belief that evil things cannot abide seeing their own images, and can therefore be stopped in their tracks and repelled by representations of themselves – a belief which probably explains the presence in churches and elsewhere of hideous faces with protruding tongues, monsters with bulging eyes and prominent teeth, and even devils and imps.

Christ himself taught in parables, using familiar objects and situations to bring some point home to his listeners. The Christian Church was quick to attach new meanings to virtually any object, bird, animal, flowers, colour or number that could possibly be exploited to reinforce its teachings. A very early example is provided

A modern Okeanus! A fish-shop sign in Carcassonne, France.
Unlike the classical Okeanus, his modern counterpart is disgorging.
Photo: Mercia MacDermott.

by St Ambrose, who lived during the fourth century, and was possibly the author of the Athanasian Creed. He urged Christians to see the waning of the Moon as an expression of its suffering while waiting for their redemption. Some such symbolic associations became a permanent part of Christian culture; others did not gain universal acceptance, or were soon forgotten. Mediaeval and post-Renaissance paintings are full of symbolic details, most of which now have to be pointed out and explained to modern viewers. For those who are aware of the message that a pearl, an egg, or a musical instrument, for example, would have conveyed to the artist's contemporaries, even Vermeer's serene domestic interiors are full of moralizing Christian symbolism.

Much of the symbolism of past centuries is now a dead language known only to specialists. In some cases, it has been lost entirely and, until some iconographic equivalent of the Rosetta Stone is found, we are unlikely to regain understanding of it. To a large extent this applies to the foliate heads in mediaeval churches.

A whole range of documents, such as chronicles, the proceedings of Church Councils, contracts between patrons and architects, parish records, laws, sermons, personal letters, encyclicals, etc., provide an insight into changing, often conflicting, views as to what was appropriate and seemly in places of Christian worship. All of them are silent about why foliate heads were introduced into Christian buildings and why they reappeared in an altered form in each new age of architectural style.

Journey's end and future goals

Paradoxically enough, the more subjective and preposterous current theories about the Green Man may, after all, provide us with the key to the mystery, though not quite in the way which their exponents intended! Perhaps what we are now witnessing is simply the latest round – and the first to be documented – in an often repeated, periodic rediscovery of the symbolic potential of an ancient decorative motif.

During the latter part of the twentieth century many people were finding themselves out of sympathy with established Churches and at odds with certain aspects of contemporary society, such as consumerism, the exploitation of animals, and the destruction of the natural environment, and were seeking alternative life-styles and systems of belief. For inspiration they turned to all manner of exotic and arcane sources, including folklore, witchcraft, Oriental schools of thought and practice, paganism, and 'Celtic spirituality'. All these they re-interpreted idiosyncratically and borrowed from eclectically.

The foliate head that Lady Raglan rescued from oblivion and arbitrarily associated with cherished traditions of a merrier England attracted the attentions of some more mystically inclined environmentalists who saw in it an ideal symbol for their cause. Thus the Green Man entered the twenty-first century re-incarnated as 'the Son of the Great Goddess', 'a pagan fertility symbol', 'the archetype of Man's Oneness with Nature', 'the Lord of the Greenwood', and a host of attractive, imaginative and emotive things which he could not possibly have represented in the context of earlier centuries. Mediaeval Christians did not identify themselves with untamed Nature, and would not have understood a desire to do so.

Of the many different forms taken by foliate heads relatively few match up to any of these grandiloquent titles. The Green Men of

Bamberg and Sutton Benger could well be 'Lords of the Greenwood', but most foliate heads suggest nothing of the kind. Some may even represent negative images of sinners and demons. Whether noble or repellent, they are too diverse to represent a single idea.

When it comes to emblems, art works, merchandise and such like, those who have harnessed the Green Man to their alternative 'green' ideology are generally selective in their choice of the image's many variants. The foliate heads most frequently copied and displayed are the quizzical leaf-masks and the tranquil disgorgers of greenery. The more hideous Gothic images and the impersonal, stylized Italianate heads are usually shunned. So, too, are the Romanesque 'cat-faces' with their trailing stems, despite their antiquity and pioneering role. Perhaps they are deemed insufficiently 'green' and 'manly' to be of current use!

The new cult of the Green Man may be seen as yet one more metamorphosis in the life-cycle of a symbol with a complicated ancestry and a long, chequered history. Throughout this history, foliate heads appear, like words in the mouth of Lewis Carroll's Humpty Dumpty, to have meant whatever their creators and beholders have chosen to make them mean.

Our journey of exploration has inexorably led us to the conclusion, that, in Christian Europe, the foliate head is primarily a decorative element, adapted from several more ancient sources and employed, as and when required, to convey a wide range of messages.

This conclusion fits all the known facts. However, before the Green Man yields the remaining secrets of his lineage and career, much more fieldwork and library research will have to be done.

In the meantime, he will continue to intrigue and to be 'full of surprises'.

BIBLIOGRAPHY

ALBANESE, Marilla, 2001, *Ancient India,* White Star Publishers.

ANDERSEN, Jørgen, 1977, *The Witch on the Wall,* Allen and Unwin.

ANDERSON, William, 1990, *Green Man - The Archetype of our Oneness with the Earth,* Harper Collins.

BARRON, W.R.J., 1979, *Sir Gawain and the Green Knight,* Manchester University Press.

BASFORD, Kathleen, 1978, *The Green Man,* D.S. Brewer (reprinted 1996).

BECKWITH, John, 1974, *Early Mediaeval Art,* Thames and Hudson.

BEHL, Benoy K., 1998, *The Ajanta Caves,* Thames and Hudson.

BUCKLAND, Theresa, and Juliette WOOD (eds), 1993, *Aspects of British Calendar Customs,* Sheffield Academic Press.

CAMPBELL, Joseph, 1962, *The Masks of God: Oriental Mythology,* Secker and Warburg; reprinted Arkana 1991.

CENTERWALL, Brandon S., 1977, 'The name of the Green Man', *Folklore, 108, 25–33.*

CHADWICK, Owen, 1995, *A History of Christianity,* Weidenfeld and Nicolson.

CHERRY, John, (ed), 1995, *Mythical Beasts,* British Museum Press.

COHN, Norman, 1993, *The Pursuit of the Millenium,* Pimlico.

CONANT, Kenneth John, 1973, *Carolingian and Romanesque Architecture, 800–1200,* Penguin.

CRAVEN, Roy C., 1987, *Indian Art,* Thames and Hudson.

CUNLIFFE, Barry, 1997, *The Ancient Celts,* OUP.

DAVID, Elizabeth, 1995, *Harvest of the Cold Months,* Penguin.

DOEL, Fran, and Geoff DOEL, 2001, *The Green Man in Britain,* Tempus.

DRAKE, C.S., 2001, *The Romanesque Fonts of Northern Europe and Scandinavia,* Boydell and Brewer.

DUFFY, Eamon, 1992, *The Stripping of the Altars,* Yale University.

FAENSON, Hubert, and Vladimir IVANOV , 1975, *Early Russian Architecture,* Paul Elek.

GOODY, Jack, 1993, *The Culture of Flowers,* CUP.

GREEN, Miranda, 1994, *Symbol and Image in Celtic Religious Art,* Routledge.

HARDING, Mike, 1998, *The Little Book of the Green Man,* Aurum Press.

HARTE, Jeremy, 2001, *The Green Man,* Pitkin Unichrome.

HAYWARD, Anthony, 2002, *The Green Men of Birmingham,* Kiva Publications.

HILL, Peter, 1996, *In Search of the Green Man in Northhamptonshire,* Orman Publications.

HUTTON, Ronald, 1991, *The Pagan Rituals of the Ancient British Isles,* Blackwell.

HUTTON, Ronald, 1996, *The Stations of the Sun. A History of the Ritual Year in Britain*, OUP.

JACOBUS de VORAGINE, 1993, *The Golden Legend*, (translated by William Granges Ryan), Princeton University Press.

JONES, Malcolm, 2002, *The Secret Middle Ages*, Sutton Publishers.

JUDGE, Roy, 1979, *The Jack in the Green*, D.S.Brewer and Rowman & Littlefield for the Folklore Society.

KAHN, Deborah, 1991, *Canterbury Cathedral and its Romanesque Sculpture*, Harvey Miller.

LASKO, Peter, 1972, *Ars Sacra 800-1200*, Pelican History of Art.

LE GOFF, Jacques (ed), 1997, *The Mediaeval World*, Parkgate Books.

LERNER, Robert, 1972, *The Heresy of the Free Spirit in the Later Middle Ages*, University of Notre Dame Press.

LUYARD, H.R. (ed), 1890, *Flores Historiarum*, Rolls Series.

MACDERMOTT, Mercia, 1998, *Bulgarian Folk Customs*, Jessica Kingsley Publishers.

MACKERALL, Benjamin, 1852, 'An account of the Company of St George in Norwich' in *History of Norwich*, MS 1737; reprinted in *Norfolk Archaeology* 3, 315–74; also reprinted in Norfolk Museums Service Information Sheet on the Norwich Snapdragon.

MARSHALL, John (ed), 1931, *Mohejo-Duro and the Indus Civilisation*. Vol.1, Arthur Probesthain

MEPISASHVILI, Rusudan, and Vakhtang TSINTSINADZE, 1979, *Arts of Ancient Georgia*, Thames and Hudson.

MILOVSKY, Aleksandr, 1987, *Pesn' Zhar-ptitsy*, Moscow.

NEUBECKER, Ottfried, and J.P. LITTLE, 1997, *Heraldry - Sources, Symbols and Meaning*, Tiger Books International.

OWEN, Richard, 2002 in *The Times* 30 March.

PARTNER, Peter, 1981, *The Knights Templar and their Myth*, Oxford UP.

REID, Piers Paul, 1999, *The Templars*, Weidenfeld & Nicolson.

RICE-OXLEY, L., 1934, *Oxford Renowned*, Methuen.

ROBBINS, Russell Hope (ed), 1959, *Historical Poems of the XIVth and XVth Centuries*, New York.

ROGERS, Mary, 1997, 'Crucifix and lily', *The Oxford Magazine*, Hilary issue.

ROGERS, Millard B., 1960, 'An Archeological Pilgrimage to Santiago de Compostela: Romanesque ornamentation of the 12th century suggests the probability of Indian influence', *Science*, No. 131.

ROZHNOVA, Polina, 1992, *A Russian Folk Calendar*, Moscow.

SCHAMA, Simon, 1996, *Landscape and Memory*, Fontana Press.

SEWARD, A.C., 1933–4, 'The Foliage, Flowers and Fruit of Southwell Chapter House', *Proceedings of the Cambridge Antiquarian Society*, Vol. 35.

SINGHAL, D.P., 1972, *India and World Civilization, Vol. I & II,* Sidgwick & Jackson.

STIERLIN, Henri, 2002, *Hindu India,* Taschen.

TOMAN, Rolf, (ed), 1997, *Romanesque,* Könemann.

WEIR, Anthony, and James JERMAN, 1986, *Images of Lust – Sexual Carving on Mediaeval Churches,* Batsford.

WILLSHER, Betty, 1996, *The Green Man,* Scottish Local History Journal, Vol. 37.

INDEX

References to illustrations are in
bold

Places are listed by country; places
in England are listed under England
and then by county.

Abbots, mock 21
Abelard, Peter 72
Adalbero, Bishop of Laon 120
Adam 105–6
Adonis 3–4
Adonis Gardens 4
Alcuin of York 117, 129
Al-Khidr 9, 14–15
amphisbaena 128
Andersen, Jørgen 132
Anderson, William 5, 63, 146, 160
Anglo-Saxon art 129, 166, **167**,
    184–5
antlers 160, 163; see also
    Cernunnus
Apollo 40
Aragon, Catherine of 70
Arcadia 42
Arminius 66
Artemisia 88, **97**
As You Like It 66
Athene – see Pallas Athene
Attis 3
Aubrey, John 38
Augustodunensis, Honorius
    (Honorius of Autun) 126
Austria 118
Autun, Honorius of 126
avaritia (greed) 75

Bacchus 45, 66, 156, 159
Bankes, John 48, 49, 69
Barber, Richard 103
Baroque architecture 35, 44
Barron W.R.J. 12

Barry, Charles 29
Basford, Kathleen 5, 8, 137, 155–6,
    159
Bayeaux tapestry 128
Beatus manuscripts 130, 184–5
Beatus, Abbot of Liébana 130
Beelzebub, Triceps 92, 94
beghards 76
beguines 76, 78
Belgium, Ghent **93**
Benedictine order 137
Bernard of Clairvaux 137
Berthold of Regensberg 76
Bertilak, Sir (Green Knight) 11
bestiaries 102–4, 128, 194
biblical references 69, 78, 81, 88,
    97, 104, 105, 106, 108, 110–
    1, 112, 122, 126, 132, 140,
    142
Bingen, Hildegard of 127
Black Death 98
Bohrer, Antoine 39
Book of Durrow 129
Book of Kells 129
Botticelli 70
Brown, 'Capability' 42
Buddhist iconography 170, 173,
    186–7, **187**, 190
Bulgaria, cat-faces 146–7
    — , folk costumes 69
    — , *peperuda* 17–19
    — , poppies 188
    — , Rila Monastery 18, **62**, 63,
    146–7
    — , Rozhen Monastery 18, **19**
    — , snakes 196
    — , sowing rituals 20
    — , St George's Day customs 21
buttercups (ranunculus) 83, 86–7
byrony 87
Byzantine art 128

Caligula 62
Campbell, Joseph 108
Caravaggio 70
Carpenter, R.C. 29

Carroll, Lewis 199
cat-faces 51, 89, 96, 126, 128, 132,
    136, 144–7, 149, 159, 165,
    199
Cathars 78
Catherine of Aragon 70
Celtic art 92, 128, 166
Celtic gods 159–60, 162
Celtic metalwork 138
Celtic stone heads 162
Centerwall, Brandon S. 64
Ceres 4
Cernunnus 9–11, 160, 164
Chadwick, Owen 121
Charlemagne 81, 113–15, 116–19
Charles I, King 56
Cherry, John 127
China, Buddhism 173, 186
— , Dunhuang 186, **187**
— , Qingzhou 174, **177**
— , triple hares motif 186, **187**
Chinese art 174, 176
chrysanthemums 194
cinquefoil (potentilla) 86–7
Cistercian order 137
Civil War, English 34
Clairvaux, Bernard of 137
Clement V, Pope 165
Clovis, King 72
Cluniac order 119–20, 123, 137
Codex Egberti **139**, 140, 143, 185
Cohn, Norman 76
Cole, Edward 49
Coman, Marc du 56
Comminges, St Bertrand de 63, 108
Conant, Kenneth John 128, 130
Connery, Sean **13**
Constantine the Great 156
Coomaraswamy, Ananda K. 176
Cosmic Tree 170; *see also* tree of
    life
Council of Trent 35
Counter-Reformation 34–7
Cranach, Lucas the Elder 47
Craven, Roy C. 170
Cuchulain 14
Cunliffe, Barry 162

Dante 121
Demeter 4, 194
Denmark – *see* Viking
Diana 40
Dick Fools 65
Dionysus 9, 23, 159
dissolution of the monasteries 34
Distillers' Company 65–6
Doel, Fran and Geoff 6
dog 96
donkey 102
dragon93, 176, 104
Druids 38
Dumuzi 3

Easter sepulchre 98–9, **100**
Egbert, Archibishop of Trier 139–
    40, 166, 185; *see also* Codex
    Egberti
Elizabeth I, Queen 34, 64
elves 4
Elwood, James 24
England, gardens 42
England [places by county:]
Avon, Bath 158, 160
Berks, Hust **67**
Buckinghamshire, Leckhampstead
    106
— , Reading 145–6
Cambridgeshire, Castor 146
— , Ely 108
— , Sutton **127**
Cheshire, Chester 49, **185**
— , Little Moreton 54
Co. Durham, Durham 72
Cumbria, Cartmel 94–5, **98**
Derbyshire, Castleton 9
— , Haddon 96
— , Hermit's Cave near Robin
    Hood's Stride 106
— , Melbourne **130**, **131**, 132,
    154
Devon, Chagford **94**, 186
— , Cheriton Bishop 186
— , Exeter 49, 88, 91, **97**, 106,
    107, 108
— , Luppitt **116**

— , Marwood, **33**
— , North Bovey 186
— , Sampford Courtenay 98, 186
— , South Tawton 98, **185**, 186
— , Spreyton 186
— , Tavistock 186
— , Widecombe 186
Dorset, Kingston Lacy 52
— , Maiden Newton **45**
Gloucestershire, Avening **6**
— , Elkstone 144
— , Cirencester 160
— , Gloucester **99**, 156
Hampshire, Stansted Park 52
— , Winchester 49
Herefordshire, Bosbury 70
— , Kilpeck **133**, 150, **150–1**,
    152, 154, **178,** 179
Kent, Canterbury 97, 126, 128,
    144–5
— , Ightham Mote 70
— , Knole 56
— , Lullington 190
— , Rochester **16**
— , Shatterling **67**
Lancashire, Whalley 94
Lincolnshire, Harpswell 100, 157
— , Heckington 99
— , Irnham 99
— , Lincoln 82–3, 99
— , Navenby **99**
London, Ham 56
— , Hampton Court 60, **60**
— , Italian fashion 60
— , May Day customs 16
— , Mortlake 56
— , St Paul's Cathedral 60
— , Whitelands College 29
Norfolk, Blickling 56
— , Norwich 64–5, **65, 79**, 96–7,
    162, **162**
— , Norwich Snapdragon 65
— , Rackheath **67**
— , Sandringham 52, **53**
Northamptonshire, Boughton 56
— , Canons Ashby 53
— , Finedon **2**

— , Kettering 157, 162
— , Northampton **117, 129**
— , Wilbarston 162
Nottinghamshire, Hawton 98, **100**
— , Southwell 82–8, **84–6, 88,**
    95–6, 101
Oxfordshire, Abingdon 110
— , Aston Tirrold **25**
— , Blenheim 60
— , Fritwell **121**
— , Oxford **46, 48**, 69, **74**, 95–6,
    97–8, 100, 101, **103**, 108,
    195
Shropshire, Linley 144
— , Much Wenlock 146, 181,
    181
— , Stokesay 54, 56, **57**
— , Stottesdon 146, **147**
Somerset, Bicknoller **77**
Suffolk, Long Melford 186
— , Mildenhall 158
Surrey, Gatton **93**
Sussex, Chichester 91, **92**, 100
— , Lancing **28**, 29
— , Southover **123**
Warwickshire, Kenilworth 64
West Midlands, Aston 56
— , Birmingham 29
Wiltshire, Salisbury 96, **101**
— , Sutton Benger 84, 192
— , Wilton House 54
Yorkshire, Beverley **112**, 186
— , Bolton 95, **95**
— , Fountains Abbey 137
— , Rievaulx 137
— , Ripon **73**
— , Sheffield 108, **109, 111**
— , Temple Newsam 58
— , Tickhill 134
— , Wintringham **24**
— , York 96
English Civil War 34
Enkidu 64
Enlightenment 37
Erigena, John Scotus 126
Essen, Mathilde of 140
Etymologies (Origines) 126

Excalibur 10
exhibitionists **130**, 131–6, **131**,
 133, 154

Faenson, Hubert 146
fairies 4
Fay, Morgan le 11
Fernando (Ferdinand), King 140
Ferrucci, Andrea 46
fir cones 153–4, 168, 172, 176
flower faces 96
folk customs 7, 9, 15–16, 17–18,
 19–22, 64–5, 68–9, 193–4
forest spirits 4
France, Abbeville 115
—, Aix-en-Provence 124
—, Amiens 124
—, Arles 124
—, Aulnay-de-Saintonge 136,
 143–4
—, Autun **152**, 154
—, Bayeaux tapestry 128
—, Beaulieu-sur-Dordogne 142
—, Bordeaux **front cover,** 124
—, Brioude **135**, **145**
—, Cahors 124, 142
—, Carcassonne 124, 176,**197**
—, Castres 61
—, Caudebec-en-Caux **5**
—, Centula 115
—, chair back **59**
—, Chambéry 124
—, Chambord 54
—, Chartes 82, 91, 96, 124
—, Chateauroux 124
—, Clermont-Ferrand **35**, 124
—, Cluny 119–20, 124, 145
—, Comminges 108
—, Conques 124
—, Dax 124
—, Dijon 75, 148, **148**
—, Dol-de-Bretagne **41**
—, Fécamp **39**
—, Fréjus 124
—, gardens 40
—, Gothic architecture 71–3
—, Irish monks travelling in 129

—, Issoire **119**
—**,** Jumièges **82**
—, La Charité-sur-Loire 124
—, Langres 124
—, Laon 120, 124
—, Le Puy 124
—, Leon 82
—, Lescar 125
—, Limoges 124
—, Luxeuil 129
—, Lyon 124, 186
—, Metz **27**, 136
—, Moissac 120, 124, 142, **143**,
 160, **161**, 179, **180**
—, Montelimar 124
—, Montpellier 124
—, Narbonne 124
—, Neuvy-Saint-Sepulcre 124
—, Nevers **32**
—, Nîmes 124
—, Noyon 84
—, Orleans 124
—, Paris 56, 72
—, Paris, Saint-Denis 124, 158
—, Périgueux 124
—, pilgrimage routes 124–5, 132
—, Poitiers 58, 124, 144, **153**,
 156–7, **159**, 176
—, Reims 82, 88, 92, 124
—, Rocamadour 124
—, Roncevalles 124
—, Rue Champeaux **7**
—, Sainte 144
—, Saintes 124
—, Saint-Gille-du-Gard 124
—, Saint-Jean-d'Angély 124
—, Saint-Léonard-de-Noblat 124
—, Saint-Sever 124
—, Saône-et-Loire 136, **152**
—, saying 66
—, Sées **36**
—, St Martin-de-Boscherville
 125
—, St Wandrille **128**
—, St-Riquier 115–6
—, Toulouse 125, **179**, 184
—, Tours 124, 129

— , triple hare motif 186
— , Troyes **7**, 124
— , Valence 124
— , Vaux-le-Vicomte 40
— , Versailles 35, 40
— , Vézelay 120, 124
— , Villefranche-de-Rouergue **90**
Francesca, Piero della 105
François I, King 54, **55**
Frazer, Sir James 9
Free Spirits 78
friars 75–6

Ganesha **183**
gardens 38, 40, 42, 68, 80–2
Garland, Castleton 9
Garland, May Day 2, 15, 87
Gawain, Sir 7, 11–14
George II, King 61
Georgia, 'green' bull's head 148
— , Mtskheta 148
— , Tbilisi 148
Germanic art 166
Germany, Aachen 114–5, 118
— , Bamberg 89, 198
— , Brunswick 66
— , Celtic stone heads 162
— , Domvorhalle **149**
— , Frankfurt 66
— , Freiburg in Breisgau 99–100
— , Gernrode 142, 154
— , Goslar 149, **149**, 150
— , Gothic architecture 71
— , Henry I 117
— , Irish monks travelling in 129
— , Magdeburg 82
— , nationalism (C16 onwards) 66, 68
— , Naumburg 82
— , Neumagen 156
— , Otto the Great 117–18
— , Pfalzfeld 162
— , Pomerania, Dukes of 66
— , Prussia, Kings of 66
— , Quedlinburg 149
— , Renaissance Green Men 47
— , Schwarzburg 66

— , Spieskappel 149–50
— , Teutoburg Forest 66, 68
— , Trier **114**, 115, 139–40, 156, 186
— , triple hare motif 186
Gerrarde, Willia 49
Gilgamesh 64
Gorgon 158
Gospel of Nicodemus 105
Gothic architecture 71–112
Gothic Green Men 159, 181, 199
Gothic Revival 26
grapes 23, 84, 97, 153
Greco, El 56, 58
Green Knight – *see* Sir Gawain
Green, Miranda 92, 160
Gregory I, Pope 121
griffins 126, 165
Grosseteste, Robert 72
Guinevere, Queen 11
Gundestrup cauldron 160
Gundrada **123**

Hadrian, Emperor 40, 115
hallowe'en 193
Harding, Mike 5–6
hares, triple 185–187, **185**, **187**
Harford, Richard 70
harpy 108
Harrington, William 100, 157
Harte, Jeremy 6
Harvy, Anthony 49
hawthorn 83, 86–7, 97
Hayward, Anthony 29
hei tiki 132
Henri II, King 40
Henri IV, King 40
Henry I, Emperor of Saxony 117
Henry I, King 145
Henry VI Part 1 4
Henry VIII, King 34, 70
Hercules 64
Hermann (Arminius) 66
Herne the Hunter 9
Herodotus 64
Hicks, Clive 5
Hildegard of Bingen 127

Hindu iconography 170
Hindu legends 169, 182
holly 164
Holmes, Sherlock 24
Holte, Sir Thomas 56
Holy Land 106, 124, 184
Honnecourt, Villard de 2, 102
hops 87
Horus 23
Hutton, Ronald 9, 21–2, 164

India, Ajanta **172**
— , Besgnagar 170, **171**
— , Bharhut stupa **174**
— , Bhopal 170
— , Bombay (Mumbai) 172
— , Chola bronzes 170
— , early churches 182
— , Hindu legends 169
— , Mumbai (Bombay) 172
— , Sanchi (Great Stupa) 172, **173**, 179
— , Tanjore (Thanjavur) **175**
Indian art 169–85
inn signs 65–6, **67**
Ireland, connections with Charlemagne 116
— , illuminated manuscripts 138
— , monks 129
— , triple heads 92
Islamic art 128
Israel, Jerusalem 106, 124, 184
Italianate architecture 29, 44, 52, 61
Italianate fashion in London 60
Italianate Green Men 46, 68, 89, 158, 199
Italy, Arezzo 105
— , Bobbio 129
— , connections with Charlemagne 116, 118
— , Cremona 76
— , Florence 46, 48, 52, 54, 70
— , fountains 52
— , gardens 38, 40
— , Genoa 104, 129
— , Gothic architecture 71

— , Herculaneum 45, 54
— , Irish monks travelling in 129
— , Italianate architecture 44
— , Medici family 38, 40, 48
— , Monte Casino 119
— , Paestrum 70, 196
— , Piacenza 129
— , Pompeii 44–5, 54
— , Pomposa 153
— , Ravenna 115, 155, 157
— , Renaissance architecture 33, 45
— , Rivolta d'Adda 136
— , rock art 160
— , Rome 40, 48, 49
— , St Homobonus 76
— , Tuscania 93
— , Udine 140
— , Val Camonica 160
— , Venice 58
— , Venitian chair **59**
— , Verona 52
Ivanov, Vladimir 146
ivy 66, 83–4, 87, 102, 164

Jack-in-the-Green 1–2, 9, 15–16, **16**
Jacobean architecture 56
Jacobean furniture 58
Jain iconography 173
James, Thomas 41
Jerman, James 132
Jesse, Tree of 106
Jesuits 35
Jones, Malcolm 132
Judge, Roy 15–16
Julius II, Pope 48
Juste, Antoine and Jean 41

Kahn, Deborah 145
Kali 23
Kama 170
King Arthur 9–11
kirttimukha 169–85, 187
Knights Templar 165–6
Koran 14

Lakshmi 182
Lasko, Peter 140
Last Judgement 121, 129–30, 142, **143**, 185
Le Goff, Jacques 75
Leo III, Pope 113
León cross 140, **141**
Lerner, Robert 76
lilies 108
Lindisfarne Gospels 129
lion 96, 102
Lord of Misrule 21
Lorrain, Claude 42
lotus 153, 172, 176, 181
Louis VI, King 72
Louis XIV, King 35, 40
lust 131
Luther, Martin 34, 47, 69, 157
luxuria (debauchery) 75

Mackerell, Benjamin 65
Maid Marion 9
makara 170–85, 187
Malory, Sir Thomas 11, 22
Malta, Adonis gardens 4
— , Mdina 61
— , Rabat 61
— , Valetta 61
manticore 127, 165
Maori 132
maple 86–7
Marshall, John 108
masques de feuilles (leaf-masks) 2
masques feuillus (foliate masks) 2
Mathilde of Essen 140
Maurus, Rabanus 110
May blossom – *see* hawthorn
May Day customs 15, 19–22, 29, 193
May King 2, 9, 19–22
Medici family 38, 40, 48
Meditationes Vitae Christi 110
Medusa 63, 158
memento mori 96
Mercury 160
Merlemont, Oliver de 152
mermaid **135**, 136

Michaelangelo 48
Middlesex, Hampton Court 60, **60**
Midgely, Graham 194
Minerva 160
Minghetti, Angelo 62
Mithras 23
mock abbots 21
monasteries, rise of 118–22; *see also* friars
Mongolian coins and metalwork 186
Moore, Temple 24
Morris dancers 9
Morris, William 26, 84
mugwort 88, 97

nature, attitudes towards 80–2
Neptune 45
Netherlands 118
New Zealand, *hei tiki* 132
Nicetius of Trier 115
Nordic art 166
'Norman' architecture – *see* Romanesque
Nôtre, André le 40, 42
Norwegian art 128, 190, **190**

oak 86–7, 97
Odo, Abbot of Cluny 119
Okeanus 44, 45, 155–6, 158, **197**
Oliba, Abbot of Ripoll 128
Olympias 196
Osiris 3, 9, 23
Otto the Great 117–18
Ovid 117
Owen, Richard 166

pagan religions and deities 3–4, 23–4, 157–65
Pallas Athene 23, 62
Pan 9, 23, 52, 64
Pantaenus 182
Paradise 79
Partner, Peter 166
Parvati 169
Peasants' Revolt 22
peperuda (Bulgarian custom) 17–19

Persephone 70
Perseus 158
Persia 127
Philip IV, King 165
Physiologus 102–3
pilgrimages 122–5, 132
pine cones – *see* fir cones
Planche, François de la 56
Pliny the Elder 64
Pliny the Younger 38
Plough Monday 19
Pomerania, Dukes of 66
poppies and poppy heads 76, **77,** 93, 96, 194
Portugal 118
Poseidon 44
potentilla spp. 86–8
Poussin, Nicola 42
protection against evil 69
Prussia, Kings of 66
pub signs 65–6, **67**
Pugin, A.W.N. 26, 29
Purgatory 76, 122

Ra 23
rabbits – *see* hares
Raglan, Lady 1, 2, 9, 15, 19, 198
Rahu 169
ranunculus (buttercups) 83, 86–7
Raymond IV 184
Reformation 34
Regensberg, Berthold of 76
Reid, Piers Paul 166
Renaissance architecture 31–4, 45, 54, 58, 73
Renaissance Green Men 68, 159
Rice-Oxley, L. 100
Robert the Pious, King 126
Robin Hood 9–11, 22
rock art, prehistoric 160
Rococco 37
Rogers, Mary 110
Rogers, Millard B. 176, 184
Roman art 128
Romanesque Green Men 51, 113–54, 164, **180,** 181, **181;** *see also* cat-faces

Romanticism 37–8
rose 87
Ruskin, John 26, 29–30
Russia, churches (C12–C13) 146
— , May Day customs 21
— , Romanesque foliate heads 147
— , St George's Day customs 20
— , Vladimir 146
— , Vsevolod III 146
— , Yurev-Polsky 146

St Abre 156–7
St Ambrose 196–7
St Augustine of Hippo 121
St Benedict 119
St Benedict of Aniane 119
St Bernard 142, 165
St George 9, 63
St George's Day 20, 65
St Hilaire (Hilary) 156
St Homobonus 76
St Isidore of Seville 126
St Jerome 117
St Michael **62,** 63, 105
St Mina 63
St Thomas 182
Sancha, Queen 140
Schama, Simon 68
Scotland, Aberdeen 52
— , Edinburgh 50, 162
— , Rosslyn Chapel (Roslin) 162, **163**
— , tombs and memorials 49–51, **50, 51**
— , Tranent 50, **50, 51**
— , triple heads 92
Scott, Gilbert 29
Scythia 126
Serbia, Studenica Monastery 147
Seth 105
Seward, A.C. 84–7
Sforza, Ascania 49
Shakespeare, William 4, 66
sheela-na-gig – *see* exhibitionists
Shiva 23, 169, 196
Shiva Natarja 170

Silenus 45
Silk Road 186, **188**, 189
Silvanus 158–9, 162
silverweed 88
Singhal, D.P. 182
Sixtus IV, Pope 110
Spain, Astorga 125
— , Barcelona 128
— , Baroque architecture 44
— , Beatus manuscripts 130, 184–5
— , Burgos 125
— , Carrion de los Condes 125
— , Catalonia 130
— , Catrogeriz 125
— , connections with Charlemagne 116, 118
— , Córdoba **43**, 44, 184
— , Ecija 61
— , Estella 125
— , Fernando (King) 140
— , Frómista 125, 136
— , Granada 47, 61, 184
— , Güejar Sierra 61
— , Indian influences on C12 churches 176–8
— , Jaca 125
— , Jerez 61
— , León 124–5
— , León cross 140, **141**
— , Liébana 130
— , Longroño 125
— , Madrid 140
— , Malaga 61
— , Moorish invasion 184
— , Najera 125
— , Oviedo 124
— , Pamploma 124
— , pilgrimage routes 124–5, 132
— , Puente la Reina 124
— , Puerto de Somport 125
— , Renaissance Green Men 46
— , Ripoll 128, 130, 143
— , Sahagún 125
— , Saint-Genis-des-Fonataines 130
— , Salamanca 147, 150
— , Sancha (Queen) 140
— , Santa Maria abbey 143
— , Santander 130
— , Santiago de Compostela 124, 132, 140, 176, 182
— , Seville 45, 46, **47**, 54, 61, 184
— , Toledo 184
— , Villafranca del Bierzo 125
Speculum Ecclesiae 126
Stratford, Robert 100
Stukeley, William 38
Stuttgarter Passionale **138**
Sucellus 162
Suger, Abbot 72
Sulis Minerva 158–9
Summer King 22
swastika 190
Sweden, Romanesque font 189–90, **189**
— , Royal Arms 66
Switzerland, Berne 124
— , Lucerne 124
— , Luzern 124
— , Reichenau 139–40
— , St Gall 129
— , triple hare motif 186
Sword of the Valiant **13**

Tacitus 66
Tammuz 3, 9
têtes de feuilles (leaf heads) 2
The Golden Legend 104
Theodoric, King 157
Theodosius I, Emperor 106
Thor 23
Tibet, spread of Buddhism 173
Tibetan art 176
Tijou, Jean 60
Tintoretto 58, 157
Toman, Rolf 128, 142–4, 150, 154
tongue pokers 111–12
Tower, Walter 29
Tree of Jesse 19, 106
tree of life 153, 162
tree, symbolism of 4
trefoils 162

triple-heads (tricephaloi) 91–5
Tucingo, Uomobuono 76
Turkey, Istanbul 155
— , Mudanya 155

Varuna 170
Varus, Publius Quintilius 66
Vasari, Girogio 71
vegetation gods 3
Vermeer, Jan 197
Viking art 138, 187–90
— , trade routes 187–90, **188**
vines 84, 87, 97, 153
Viollet-le-Duc, E. 176–7
Virgil 117
Vishnu 23
Vision of St Paul 121
Volpiano, William of 149
Voragine (Voraigne), Jacobus de
    104–5
Vsevolod III, Prince 146

Wales, Haverfordwest 80
— , Powis 54
— , Tintern 137
Weir, Anthony 132
whifflers 64
White, T.S. 103
Wild Man 63–8
Wildman of the Woods 63
William and Mary 60
William of Volpiano, Abbot 149
Willsher, Betty 51
Wish-fulfilling Tree 170
Woden 166
woodwose 63–8, **65**
world tree 4
wormwood 88, 97
Wren, Sir Christopher 60
wyvern 128, 154, 181
yakshi 170, **171**
Yeti 64

Zeus 23, 44

Also from Heart of Albion Press

The *Explore* series provides accessible introductions to folklore and mythology. Some books provide 'overviews' of quite broad topics, drawing together current academic research with popular beliefs. Other books in the series deal with more specific topics, but still with the aim of providing a wide-ranging introduction to the topic.

Already published:

Explore Folklore
Bob Trubshaw

Explore Mythology
Bob Trubshaw

Explore Shamanism
Alby Stone

Explore Fairy Traditions
Jeremy Harte

Explore Phantom Black Dogs
edited by Bob Trubshaw

Explore Hinduism
Bansi Pandit

Explore Dragons
Richard Freeman

Explore Mythology

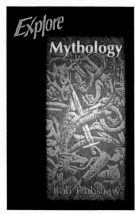

Bob Trubshaw

Myths are usually thought of as something to do with 'traditional cultures'. The study of such 'traditional' myths emphasises their importance in religion, national identity, hero-figures, understanding the origin of the universe, and predictions of an apocalyptic demise. The academic study of myths has done much to fit these ideas into the preconceived ideas of the relevant academics.

Only in recent years have such long-standing assumptions about myths begun to be questioned, opening up whole new ways of thinking about the way such myths define and structure how a society thinks about itself and the 'real world'.

These new approaches to the study of myth reveal that, to an astonishing extent, modern day thinking is every bit as 'mythological' as the world-views of, say, the Classical Greeks or obscure Polynesian tribes. Politics, religions, science, advertising and the mass media are all deeply implicated in the creation and use of myths.

Explore Mythology provides a lively introduction to the way myths have been studied, together with discussion of some of the most important 'mythic motifs' – such as heroes, national identity, and 'central places' – followed by a discussion of how these ideas permeate modern society. These sometimes contentious and profound ideas are presented in an easily readable style of writing.

ISBN 1 872883 62 1
Perfect bound. Demi 8vo (215 x 138 mm), 220 + xx pages, 17 line drawings. **£9.95**

Explore Folklore

Bob Trubshaw

'A howling success, which plugs a big and obvious gap'
Professor Ronald Hutton

There have been fascinating developments in
the study of folklore in the last twenty-or-so
years, but few books about British folklore and folk customs reflect
these exciting new approaches. As a result there is a huge gap
between scholarly approaches to folklore studies and 'popular
beliefs' about the character and history of British folklore. *Explore
Folklore* is the first book to bridge that gap, and to show how much
'folklore' there is in modern day Britain.

Explore Folklore shows there is much more to folklore than morris
dancing and fifty-something folksingers! The rituals of 'what we do
on our holidays', funerals, stag nights and 'lingerie parties' are all full
of 'unselfconscious' folk customs. Indeed, folklore is something that
is integral to all our lives – it is so intrinsic we do not think of it as
being 'folklore'.

The implicit ideas underlying folk lore and customs are also
explored. There might appear to be little in common between
people who touch wood for luck (a 'tradition' invented in the last
200 years) and legends about people who believe they have been
abducted and subjected to intimate body examinations by aliens.
Yet, in their varying ways, these and other 'folk beliefs' reflect the
wide spectrum of belief and disbelief in what is easily dismissed as
'superstition'.

Explore Folklore provides a lively introduction to the study of most
genres of British folklore, presenting the more contentious and
profound ideas in a readily accessible manner.

ISBN 1 872883 60 5
Perfect bound, demi 8vo (215x138 mm), 200 pages, **£9.95**

Also from Heart of Albion Press

Winner of the Folklore Society's Katahrine Briggs Award 2005

Explore Fairy Traditions

Jeremy Harte

We are not alone. In the shadows of our countryside there lives a fairy race, older than humans, and not necessarily friendly to them. For hundreds of years, men and women have told stories about the strange people, beautiful as starlight, fierce as wolves, and heartless as ice. These are not tales for children. They reveal the fairies as a passionate, proud, brutal people.

Explore Fairy Traditions draws on legends, ballads and testimony from throughout Britain and Ireland to reveal what the fairies were really like. It looks at changelings, brownies, demon lovers, the fairy host, and abduction into the Otherworld. Stories and motifs are followed down the centuries to reveal the changing nature of fairy lore, as it was told to famous figures like W.B. Yeats and Sir Walter Scott. All the research is based on primary sources and many errors about fairy tradition are laid to rest.

Jeremy Harte combines folklore scholarship with a lively style to show what the presence of fairies meant to people's lives. Like their human counterparts, the secret people could kill as well as heal. They knew marriage, seduction, rape and divorce; they adored some children and rejected others. If we are frightened of the fairies, it may be because their world offers an uncomfortable mirror of our own.

ISBN 1 872883 61 3.
Perfect bound. Demi 8vo (215 x 138 mm), 186 + vi pages, 6 line drawings, **£9.95**

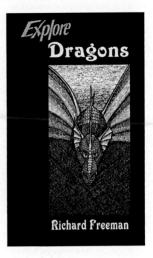

Explore Dragons

Richard Freeman

The dragon is the most ancient and widespread of all monsters. Dragon legends are told in every culture and in every continent on Earth. Its breath condenses and forms rain in China. It slithers across the heavens in Mexico as Quetzalcoatl. In Scandinavian lore its coils encircled the whole earth. No other monster is so universal in its occurrence or so varied.

But the British Isles are the homeland of the dragon. Although a small country, it is seething with dragon legends. Explore Dragons puts British dragon stories into their international context and attempts to fathom out what really lurks behind these fanciful tales. Could dragons once have been real creatures? Are such creatures still alive?

Richard Freeman is a former zookeeper and has a degree in zoology. He is the zoological director of the Centre for Fortean Zoology in Exeter. A full-time cryptozoologist, he has searched for monsters and mystery animals in Indo-China, Sumatra, and Mongolia as well as in the UK.

Published by Explore Books, an imprint of Heart of Albion Press.
EAN 978-1-872883-939. ISBN 1 872883 93 1. May 2006
Demy 8vo (215 x 138 mm), paperback.
£12.95

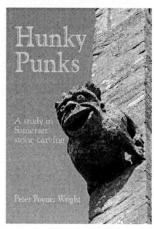

Hunky Punks
A study in Somerset stone carving

Peter Poyntz-Wright

High up on the famous church towers of Somerset, almost lost to the eye except for their silhouettes, are an amazing series of grotesque stone figures. Carved in the fifteenth and sixteenth centuries, to ornament corners and break up straight sections of masonry, these figures are known in some rural areas at hunky punks.

This book combines a fascinating historical and architectural study with a stunning collection of photographs. Peter Poyntz-Wright's research provides the first thorough account of the hunky punks and gives us a direct insight into the medieval mind. He examines the techniques and influences of the medieval masons, and considers methods of attachment and the effects of weathering.

The author has recorded a host of hitherto unknown and inaccessible medieval carvings the first time – and possibly for the last. They include such creatures as dragons, griffins, hounds, stags, heraldic creatures, a basilisk, the devil, a woman in childhood, and many others. However many of the hunk punks are suffering seriously from the effects of wearing, and some, without costly restoration, may not survive for many more years.

Peter Poyntz-Wright is author of *The Parish Church Towers of Somerset* and *The Rural Bench Ends of Somerset,* and is currently writing a biography of the early sixteenth century Somerset woodcarver, Simon Warman. He lives in Somerset and lectures widely on medieval architectural, archaeological and historical topics.

ISBN 1 872883 75 X. Spring 2004, A5, perfect bound, approx. 160 pages, 76 full page b&w photos, 3 line drawings. **£9.95**

Good Gargoyle Guide

Medieval Carvings of Leicestershire and Rutland

Bob Trubshaw

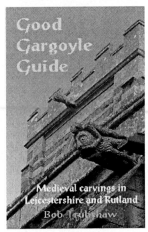

Grimacing gargoyles adorn many of the churches in Leicestershire and Rutland. Alongside them are a wide range of imaginary beasties, foliate faces and Green Men, face-pulling heads, contortionists, and other imaginative figurative carvings. While those on the outside of the churches may be badly weathered, their counterparts inside are usually near-perfect examples of the medieval mason's skills.

Leicestershire and Rutland is fortunate in having more such carvings than in adjoining counties, although this wealth of medieval art has been unjustly overlooked by church historians. These depictions provide a unique insight into the often rather disturbing thinking of the craftsmen who carved them many hundreds of years ago, people who are otherwise almost entirely invisible from historical records.

The aim of the *Good Gargoyle Guide* is to encourage people who would not normally take an interest in church architecture to get out and about hunting further examples of these extraordinary sculptures.

ISBN 1872883 70 2. March 2004. Demi 8vo (215 x 138 mm), 100 + xii pages, 151 b&w photographs, perfect bound. **£6.95**

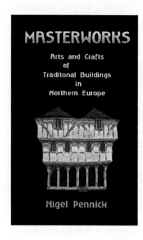

Masterworks

Arts and Crafts of Traditional Building in Northern Europe

Nigel Pennick

Masterworks is about the traditions of arts and crafts in northern Europe, taking as a starting point the use of timber in building. Timber frame buildings have been constructed over a long period of time over a large territory, mostly northern and north-west Europe. Various regional and local styles have come into being.

Timber buildings display a rich diversity of techniques, forms and patterns developed by generations of master craftsmen working with local materials under similar limitations. The 'arts and crafts' used in the construction of these buildings acknowledge and celebrate the knowledge, traditions, abilities and spiritual understanding of how to work effectively with natural materials. They are living traditions that remain relevant today.

Masterworks is a celebration of this arts and crafts ethos that is present in the traditional buildings of northern Europe.

> "*Masterworks* ... is written by a man who is not only in tune with his subject matter but is, in fact, a master wordsmith in his own right and deserves credit for this. I personally found this one of his most intriguing and important works to date and cannot recommend it too highly to the discerning reader."
> Ian Read *Runa*

ISBN 1 872883 63 X Perfect bound, Demi 8vo, 163 + viii pages, 23 b&w photos, 15 line drawings **£9.95**

A Bestiary of Brass

Peter Heseltine

From antelopes to wyverns, with over fifty species in between, *A Bestiary of Brass* looks the animals, birds, insects, fish – even shellfish – which have been depicted on medieval memorial brasses in Britain. Some are native, others – such as elephants and panthers – were exotic, while dragons and unicorns were as mythical then as they are today.

At the time they were engraved these creatures evoked a wide range of folklore and legends. This rich symbolism is brought to life by the author. But enigmas remain – why would anyone want to be associated with a fox when they were more noted for cunning and slyness, or a hedgehog, or even a whelk? We also find out about the lives of the people commemorated and share the author's detailed knowledge of their heraldic emblems. Practical advice is provided to help make brass rubbings and to learn more about these memorials.

The illustrations show a wide range of the memorials, with detailed views of the creatures they incorporate. *A Bestiary of Brass* will appeal to anyone interested in folklore, art and medieval history. Above all, these masterpieces of craftsmanship reveal that our deep fascination with animals was shared by our ancestors many hundreds of years ago.

EAN 978 1872 883 908. ISBN 1 872883 90 7. March 2006.
Demy 8vo (215 x 138 mm), over 280 illustrations, paperback
£12.95

Taliesin's Travels

A demi-god at large

Michael Dames

Taliesin's Travels brings fresh significance to one of Britain's best-loved tales.

For over a thousand years the impish Taliesin has enthralled and enlightened people. As a farmer's son, he is grounded in the land. Yet, because his mother is the goddess Nature, he can travel, free as a demi-god, throughout time and space.

Thanks to his intimate contact with spirits of place, sun and underworld, Taliesin reveals and portrays the interconnecting, ever-transforming essence of life. His often painful and sometimes ludicrous adventures engage with creation in its entirety. Transcending history, he invites us to see our own millennium as a cyclical, mythic journey so that, like him, each individual comes to identify with the whole of creation.

With a keen sense of enjoyment, Michael Dames provides a deep and imaginative account of the tales and poetry associated with Taliesin. Prehistoric, Romano-British and Christian aspects of Taliesin's persona are brought together in a magical synthesis.

Michael Dames is well-known for his pioneering studies of the myths and legends of the British Isles. His previous books include *The Silbury Treasure, The Avebury Cycle, Mythic Ireland* and *Merlin and Wales.*

EAN 978 1872 883 892. ISBN 1 872883 89 3. February 2006.
245 x 175 mm, over 200 illustrations, paperback £16.95

The Enchanted Land

Myths and Legends of Britain's Landscape

Revised, fully illustrated edition

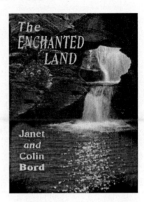

Janet and Colin Bord

Britain's landscape is overlain by a magic carpet of folklore and folktales, myths and legends. Enchantment and legend still lurk in places as diverse as hills and mountains, rivers and streams, caves and hollows, springs and wells, cliffs and coasts, pools and lakes, and rocks and stones.

The dramatic stories woven around these places tell of sleeping knights, beheaded saints, giants, dragons and monsters, ghosts, King Arthur, mermaids, witches, hidden treasure, drowned towns, giant missiles, mysterious footprints, visits to Fairyland, underground passages, human sacrifices, and much more.

The 'Places to Visit' section locates and describes in detail more than 50 sites.

This revised edition is fully illustrated, with around 130 photographs and illustrations.

Janet and Colin Bord live in North Wales, where they run the Fortean Picture Library. They have written more than 20 books since their first successful joint venture, *Mysterious Britain* in 1972.

From reviews of the first edition:

'Janet's own enthusiasm for a number of the sites is conveyed vividly and lends credibility to the notion that Britain is still an enchanted land.' *Mercian Mysteries*

ISBN 1 872883 91 5. March 2006. 245 x 175 mm, over 200 illustrations, paperback **£16.95**

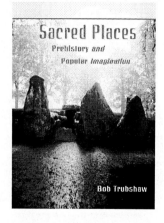

Sacred Places:

Prehistory and popular imagination

Bob Trubshaw

Sacred Places asks why certain types of prehistoric places are thought of as sacred, and explores how the physical presence of such sacred sites is less important than what these places signify. So this is not another guide book to sacred places but instead provides a unique and thought-provoking guide to the mental worlds – the mindscapes – in which we have created the idea of prehistoric sacred places.

Recurring throughout this book is the idea that we continually create and re-create our ideas about the past, about landscapes, and the places within those landscapes that we regard as sacred. For example, although such concepts as 'nature', 'landscape', 'countryside', 'rural' and the contrast between profane and sacred are all part of our everyday thinking, in this book Bob Trubshaw shows they are all modern cultural constructions which act as the 'unseen' foundations on which we construct more complex myths about places.

Key chapters look at how earth mysteries, modern paganism and other alternative approaches to sacred places developed in recent decades, and also outline the recent dramatic changes within academic archaeology. Is there now a 'middle way' between academic and alternative approaches which recognises that what we know about the past is far less significant than what we believe about the past?

Bob Trubshaw has been actively involved with academic and alternative approaches to archaeology for most of the last twenty years. In 1996 he founded *At the Edge* magazine to popularise new interpretations of past and place.

ISBN 1 872883 67 2. Published 2005.
245 x 175 mm, 203 + xiv pages, 43 b&w illustrations and 7 line drawings, paperback. **£16.95**

Also from Heart of Albion Press

Stonehenge:
Celebration and Subversion

Andy Worthington

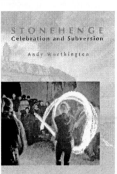

This innovative social history looks in detail at
how the summer solstice celebrations at
Stonehenge have brought together different
aspects of British counter-culture to make the monument a 'living
temple' and an icon of alternative Britain. The history of the
celebrants and counter-cultural leaders is interwoven with the
viewpoints of the land-owners, custodians and archaeologists who
have generally attempted to impose order on the shifting patterns of
these modern-day mythologies.

The story of the Stonehenge summer solstice celebrations begins with
the Druid revival of the 18th century and the earliest public gatherings
of the 19th and early 20th centuries. In the social upheavals of the
1960s and early 70s, these trailblazers were superseded by the
Stonehenge Free Festival. This evolved from a small gathering to an
anarchic free state the size of a small city, before its brutal
suppression at the Battle of the Beanfield in 1985.

In the aftermath of the Beanfield, the author examines how the
political and spiritual aspirations of the free festivals evolved into both
the rave scene and the road protest movement, and how the
prevailing trends in the counter-culture provided a fertile breeding
ground for the development of new Druid groups, the growth of
paganism in general, and the adoption of other sacred sites, in
particular Stonehenge's gargantuan neighbour at Avebury.

The account is brought up to date with the reopening of Stonehenge
on the summer solstice in 2000, the unprecedented crowds drawn by
the new access arrangements, and the latest source of conflict,
centred on a bitterly-contested road improvement scheme.

ISBN 1 872883 76 1. Published 2004. Perfect bound, 245 x 175 mm,
281 + xviii pages, 147 b&w photos, **£14.95**

Heart of Albion

The UK's leading publisher of folklore, mythology and cultural studies.

Further details of all Heart of Albion titles online at
www.hoap.co.uk

All titles available direct from Heart of Albion Press.
Please add £1.30 p&p (UK only; email
albion@indigogroup.co.uk for overseas postage).

To order books or request our current catalogue please
contact

Heart of Albion Press
2 Cross Hill Close, Wymeswold
Loughborough, LE12 6UJ

Phone: 01509 880725
Fax: 01509 881715
email: albion@indigogroup.co.uk
Web site: www.hoap.co.uk